G.R.A.C.E.

▼

The Essence of Spirituality

Dennis R. Fakes

Writer's Showcase

San Jose New York Lincoln Shanghai

G.R.A.C.E.
The Essence of Spirituality

Writer's Showcase
an imprint of iUniverse, Inc.

For information address:
iUniverse, Inc.
5220 S. 16th St., Suite 200
Lincoln, NE 68512
www.iuniverse.com

ISBN: 0-595-22724-4

Printed in the United States of America

G.R.A.C.E.

ACKNOWLEDGMENTS

I would like to acknowledge the following for assisting me in the creation of this book: the people of St. Paul Lutheran Church for their on-going encouragement in living lives of prayer and grace. I need to thank my dear wife Hilda for her strength of faith and character. Also to Janet Thompson, Jan Flanery, and Dorothy Pendleton for their personal encouragment. My daughter Cara Fakes for her helpful comments. Finally and especially to Shannon Ekeren-Moening for critiquing and proof reading the text. I could not and would not have continued the endeavor of this book without the aforementioned.

April 25, 2002

INTRODUCTION

Rejoice always, pray without ceasing, give thanks in all circumstances; for this is the will of God in Christ Jesus for you. (1 Thessalonians 5:16-18)

I amaze myself. I have always had "two left feet." I am most certainly clumsy—or, as I prefer to say, kinesthetically challenged. The word "graceful" has never described me—at least not in the way the word graceful is commonly used. But I am learning, slowly and sometimes not so surely, to live a life that is grace-full—in a way I have found describes the fullest kind of life possible.

What is grace? Like good humor, trying to define grace is to ruin it. The best way to define grace is to live in it and experience it. Grace comes when we know that we are accepted, as Paul Tillich said: "You are accepted by that which is greater than you, and the name of which you do not know."[1] Unconditionally, freely accepted. Grace has no strings attached. Grace means that I am a beautiful work of creation even if my own deep voices vehemently protest the adjective "beautiful" as self-description.

Grace too easily becomes a theological abstraction—nice in thought but of little or no practical use in daily living. While we human beings can understand abstractions, we more easily understand story and bodily postures. Prayer is the story of the soul's longing for greater reality and communication with that deeper essence—that "Higher Power." Throughout history prayer of every religious expression has had postures: folded hands, open hands, bowed head, bent knees.

To live a life of grace is to live prayerfully. The fifteenth century reformer Martin Luther said that prayer is our speaking to God and grace is God's speaking to us. "But God's speaking is more comforting than ours." In other words, grace is greater than prayer. Prayer, however, is perhaps the best means of accessing what might otherwise be a theological abstraction: grace.

Living prayerfully does not mean going around muttering prayers all day long. A prayerful life is a life lived in deep connection with one's God. The nineteenth century restorer of evangelical theology, Schleiermacher, observed, "To be religious and to pray—that is really one and the same thing." Another observer, Novalis, the poet of romanticism, put it this way, "Praying is to religious what thinking is to philosophy. Praying is religion in the making. The religious sense prays, just as the thinking mechanism thinks." Prayer and spirituality go together. Wherever one finds a deep spirituality, one will also find prayer. The life of grace is a life lived in prayer.

Too often prayer is construed as a work we do to earn God's grace. I am proposing that grace and prayer are linked and we do not earn more grace because we have longer prayers. Prayer is life—not deed. Grace is gift—not something earned. Dutch theologian and author Henri J. M. Nouwen puts it like this: "The paradox of prayer is that we have to learn how to pray while we can only receive it as a gift... All mystics stress with an impressive unanimity that prayer is 'grace,' that is, a free gift from God, to which we can only respond with gratitude."[2]

When Paul writes to the Thessalonians "Rejoice always, pray without ceasing, give thanks in all circumstances," he was not prescribing an impossible act of devotion. Taken literally, to rejoice *always*, pray *without ceasing*, and to give thanks in *all* circumstances would allow no time for sleep, work, or conversation. Paul is here describing to the Thessalonians the prayerful life of grace-full living. All of life is a prayer. All living is in the state of grace.

Prayer is the grace-response of human beings encountering the awesome mystery of God. Prayer is the expression and yearning of grace. In a sense prayer is the language of grace. It flows effortlessly, naturally, from the spring of faith, which, for all deeply religious of any persuasion is grace. Perhaps no one has put it more beautifully or succinctly than Robert Louis Stevenson: "There is nothing but God's grace. We walk upon it; we breathe it; we live and die it; it makes the nails and axles of the universe."[3]

Prayer, its various postures, and grace form a kind of trinity that expresses the ineffable spiritual language of faith.

CHAPTER ONE

▼

G.R.A.C.E.

Rejoice in the Lord always; again I will say, Rejoice. Let your gentleness be known to everyone. The Lord is near. Do not worry about anything, but in everything by prayer and supplication with thanksgiving let your requests be made known to God. And the peace of God, which surpasses all understanding, will guard your hearts and your minds in Christ Jesus.

Finally, beloved, whatever is true, whatever is honorable, whatever is just, whatever is pure, whatever is pleasing, whatever is commendable, if there is any excellence and if there is anything worthy of praise, think about these things. (Philippians 4:4-8)

Recently the news reported an incident on Lake Isabella, located in the high desert of Southern California, east of Bakersfield. It seems a certain fellow new to boating was having a problem. No matter how hard he tried, he just couldn't get his brand new 22 foot Bayliner to perform. It was sluggish in almost every maneuver, no matter how much power he supplied. After about an hour of trying to make it go, the boater puttered over to a nearby marina. Maybe they could tell him what was wrong.

A thorough topside check revealed everything was in perfect working order. The engine ran fine, the outdrive went up and down, the prop was the correct size and pitch. One of the mechanics at the marina volunteered to jump in the water to check underneath. He came up choking and sputtering because he was laughing so hard. Under the boat, still strapped securely place, was the trailer.

That incident reminds me of our human condition. How often we live our lives with the trailer still attached! We want the fullness of life. We want the beauty and joy of life, but we don't know how. Instead we spend a great deal of time and energy worrying about this or that. We tremble and fear instead of trusting and obeying. Latent anger robs our nights of sleep and our days of joy. This book is about the simple fullness of life promised by Jesus. He defined his purpose simply: "I came that they may have life, and have it abundantly."[4] The abundant life is a prayerful life of GRACE.

A grace-filled life is a life lived in the posture of PRAYER. Prayer is more than what a person *does* or *says*. In fact prayer as I am speaking of it in this book, is less what we DO and more what we ARE! GRACE-filled creatures.

Wayne (Tony) Mabes of Blue Ridge, Texas, tells a story about grace:
> As a youngster I lived in the Appalachian Mountains of West Virginia and attended the local elementary school. Money was scarce in my family, mainly because my father had been disabled in a coal mine cave-in. Christmas was a particularly painful time for my family. My parents agonized about how they could give us kids gifts for Christmas. Of course, participating in the tradition of "drawing names" in school to exchange gifts with other children

was not a possibility. For me, there were no talks with friends about who got whose name and "what were you gonna get" for that kid. I felt so left out.

But the most painful part came on the day when the long-awaited gifts were brought to school for exchange and I had none to give—and I knew that I alone would not receive a gift. I knew, as well as an eight-year old kid could know, this was just another thing that I would miss out on because my family was poor. The party started and the opening of the gifts was the first order of business. Our teacher picked up the first gift and read my name! I was so excited!

This happened three more times during my elementary years. And, years later, I found that the gifts came from Mrs. Lilly, the mother of Griffin, one of my classmates. And I was not the only child to whom she had given gifts—there were several others.

I now live far away from the hills of West Virginia and far away from the poverty I had suffered as a child. Her kindness and generosity made a deep impression on me and I try often to recognize, as she did, other people's needs and to help them as well. And in 1997, while visiting family "back home", I stopped by and thanked Mrs. Lilly personally. But now, I'd like to let the whole world know that "there's gold in them thar hills." It is Griffin Lilly's mother. [5]

Grace is such a simple concept—simple enough for an eight-year-old child to understand. It is the concept of love freely given. On a child's level that love comes in the form of a gift—undeserved, unpaid-for, and unexpected. God's grace is like Tony's gift—only on a grand scale. God's love is in the gift of life and all the goodness of life and the promise of eternal life.

And what is the response to grace? The response is Tony's response to Griffin Lilly's mother. He "stopped by and thanked Mrs. Lilly personally." Gratitude is the first response of grace in a grace-filled, prayerful life. The initial posture of a Grace-filled life is that of thankful, praying hands. The words GRACE and GRATITUDE have a common bond in our language. Both have the Latin word *gratia*, meaning "pleasing" or "out of kindness" as their root.

The Christian word "grace" means love freely given—unconditional, with no strings attached. Griffin Lilly's mother exhibited grace.

Most of us live in a world that embraces the opposite of grace—legalism. Doing right results in reward; doing wrong punishment. Even the natural world tells us that nature rewards right behavior and punishes wrong. There is no room for grace—for gift.

But grace pops up in the secular world all the time. (And legalism abounds in the religious world too much). A recent issue of U.S. News and World Report[6] had an article about a new safety-initiative at Children's Hospitals and Clinics in Minneapolis and St. Paul. The CEO, Julie Morath, required staffers to report mistakes that hurt patients or had the potential to do so.

Reporting mistakes is nothing new. That's legalism. That's what businesses are supposed to do. But this hospital had a different twist. The purpose of reporting mistakes was to identify and correct problems before they hurt another patient. That's grace. That's gift—to some anonymous and perhaps future patient. The old system of identifying mistakes in order to punish the perpetrator and protect the organization is legalism.

To encourage staff members (from physicians to janitors) to report problems, the focus at Children's Hospitals and Clinics was not on finding someone to blame but on identifying why things went wrong. "Morath hopes to assure employees that they can safely admit mistakes anonymously, without fear of punishment, allowing everyone to learn from them".[7] She says, "We're trained clinically to be perfect, but the human being is an imperfect instrument. We are just not wired to be correct 100 percent of the time".[8]

This hospital CEO is talking about grace. Morath has learned that all humans make mistakes—or do things wrong—(traditionally called "sin"). She has also discovered that, when people live in a world with no grace, they try to sweep their mistakes (sins) under the carpet where nobody will notice—or they feel so guilty that they quit medicine (as a nurse of Morath's acquaintance did). If they live in a world where there is grace, they are more apt to report the errors, which makes it possible to devise systemic solutions that prevent further error. That not only saves patients' lives, but it also makes the hospital a much more humane place for physicians, nurses, and other staff members.

If that is true in a hospital, might it also be true in a family? If parents focus on blaming a child for mistakes, doesn't that undermine the child's confidence and make the child think of herself as a failure?

For millenniums human beings have wrestled with how to deal with individuals who drink too much. Most of the time the person was shamed, dishonored, put down as weak-willed and worthless. Funny thing, however, that strategy almost never worked in helping alcoholics recover.

But sixty-some years ago a couple of individuals who also happened to be enslaved to alcohol discovered that they did not have to will themselves to recovery or prove themselves superior to the bottle. Instead they submitted and acknowledged their own inability to overcome their slavery. They substituted their own self-sufficiency and relied only on grace—the gift of a "higher power"—which could help them deal with their destructive drinking "one day at a time."

Whether in business, at home, or in the clutch of alcoholism—or in just being a human from day to day—grace is the highest gift any of us could ever receive. In fact grace is God's ultimate gift.

God exhibits grace for us in daily gifts. The very fact of being alive is a gift from God. You could be non-existent and without being because you were never conceived and born. But the fact is you *are*. You have being. You exist. Happenstance and circumstance conspired to create the being you are. Only a minute different quirk of history would have produced a different being than the one reading these words. But the reality is you ARE and that is grace. You did not ask to be conceived. You did not earn your birth. You did nothing to contribute to the fact of your being. It was all gift—grace—"love freely given."

On top of the gift of life and time itself, how many other gifts do you celebrate in this moment? You could be languishing in some prison. You could be trapped in the crumpled rubble of a wrecked automobile. But that is likely not the case—you are here!

The surest gift of GRACE is the gift of eternal life by Jesus Christ, our Lord. We didn't ask for it; we didn't earn it—it was simply and freely given. It cost Jesus everything, but the gift to you and me is unconditionally free!

The normal response is prayer and the prayer says simply: THANKS! Gratitude. When I think of gratitude, the image that immediately comes to mind is that of hands folded simply and elegantly in prayer.

As grace is unconditionally given, so it must be received. Only empty hands can receive. The second posture of grace is the posture of open hands—_R_elease. Hands that are full cannot receive. Hands must open to release non-grace things and attitudes and addictions to receive the wonderful gift of God's unconditional acceptance. Dr. Gerald G. May put it well:

> …(G)race seeks us but will not control us. Saint Augustine once said that God is always trying to give good things to us, but our hands are too full to receive them. If our hands are full, they are full of the things to which we are addicted. And not only our hands, but also our hearts, minds, and attention are clogged with addiction. Our addictions fill up the spaces within us, spaces where grace might flow.[9]

I've been told one can catch monkeys by putting food in a space large enough so the monkey can put his hand through the bars, but small enough that he cannot withdraw his fist. He puts his hand in, grabs the food and then will not let go even when a human comes along with a net to catch him.

We human beings so easily get caught in nets of unhappiness because we grab and will not let go. I am convinced that most of us are grabbing at materialism for our happiness and joy. We imagine that if we only had a little more of this or that, *then* we'd be truly happy and at peace. Of course it doesn't happen.

I can trace advancing materialism and increasing prosperity in my own community. Toward the center of town, the homes are small and many have no garage. Then as one travels out from the core, one-car garages were built and even attached to the homes. Further out two-car, attached garages seem to be the neighborhood standard. Then, still further from the core, new homes have three and four-car garages—and vehicles parked on the street because the garages are full of other possessions. Now the question I ask is this: are the affluent on the edge of town more joy-filled than those who live closer to the center? How about people of earlier times who never even knew the definition of "garage"? I doubt it. Based on substance abuse, suicide, crime and other social factors, I see no correlation between things and happiness. If anything there seems to be a correlation between things and unhappiness!

Like monkeys, grabbing at food, we grab at things and things grab us. The things we treasure when bright and new on the shelf at the store nearly always disappoint us. They did not bring the promised happiness but they did bring some degree of capture and enslavement. The posture of the grace-filled life is open hands. Open for two reasons: If we are to receive grace, then we must let go of the many things we *think* cause happiness so that we can receive the abundant, wonderful gift of grace that *really does* cause happiness and more—joy.

The accumulation of things alone is not all that weighs us down. We also burden ourselves with attitudes and emotions that weigh heavily. I was reminded of this as recently as yesterday.

Yesterday I felt another person treated me with a perceived injustice. I was angry. That anger presented me with a choice. I could hold on to it and let it corrupt my day like mold, or I could let go of the anger and receive the grace that comes from a loving God. The equation is a no-brainer. Why would anyone want to hold on to something negative and have that negativity ruin his day? No one would, but we often do. I was tempted to hang on to the injustice and enjoy the self-righteous feeling of martyrdom instead of freely living the abundant, prayerful life of grace.

To embrace that prayerful, grace-full life, hands must be empty of negative emotion. We must release the anger and disappointment or else they fill our hands and we cannot receive life's very best—grace.

The same goes for fear. As Montaigne says, "He who fears he will suffer already suffers because of his fear." Most fears are not as bad as the reality. The suffering we cause ourselves because of our fear far outpaces the reality of life's slings and arrows. Fear, like anger, needs to be dropped to the floor so our open arms can receive the abundance of grace. As the old saying so simply states: LET GO…AND LET GOD.

If releasing and emptying our hands is important in receiving grace, then so is the next part: *A*cceptance. Empty hands allow for acceptance. We can receive only when our hands are vacant. If they are full, then there is no room for more.

Part of the fullness we have in our hands is the fullness of our own expectations of what life "should" be. People *should* say this; they *should* respond in this manner instead of that. We *should* not experience this pain. We *shouldn't* have to bear this awful burden. We really *ought to have* said something other than what we did.

The ability to accept life on life's own terms is so important if one is to live the prayerful life of grace. It is important for health; for life; for the fullness and richness of existence.

The other day I was sitting on a plane in Dallas and the pilot came back to the passenger section. He knelt beside me, turned his back to me, and asked the man sitting across the aisle if he was Mr. So-and-so. I couldn't help but overhear the conversation. The pilot said, "I understand you are pretty frustrated and angry and that you gave the attendant a hard time. I will have none of this on my plane. I have the authority to have you arrested and detained. I cannot tolerate the abuse of my flight crew. Can we come to an agreement that there will be none of this behavior on this flight? Otherwise I must ask you to get off this plane now."

The flight was delayed. It was late in the day. People were tired, hungry, frustrated because of the delays. But there were also options. I noticed the man sitting across the aisle from me seemed to have a pleasant flight. I never detected a moment of anger or frustration in him throughout the rest of our journey together. I suspect the pilot's little talk enabled him to choose a more pleasant option and attitude.

Much of life's happiness and joy depends upon our accepting life on its own terms. Some wise, anonymous sage wrote: "A contented person is the one who enjoys the scenery along the detours."

Millions of people have benefited from the so-called "Serenity Prayer" that says:

> God grant me the serenity to accept the things I cannot change;
> Courage to change the things I can.
> And the wisdom to know the difference.

Acceptance of life's sometimes cold, indifferent, violent and sinister ways is important for the grace-filled life, but acceptance of grace itself is most important. Empty hands allow for such acceptance.

Acceptance of grace means letting God do the accepting. Our human nature will fight this tooth and nail. We want to save ourselves. We want to justify and excuse ourselves. We did this *because*. The *reason* we can't do better is…

Most people feel they should measure up. Madison Avenue says that if we wear the right clothing, we can indeed measure up. If we drive the right car, then perhaps we can attain value and worth. If we are physically well-proportioned, then we probably measure up. If we are old enough or young enough or have the right degree from the right college, *then* we can perhaps be worthy. Coming from the right side of town or from the right family helps one earn merit.

Wall Street would tell us that "net worth" is the true measure of a person's worth. Having the fastest-growing stock picks or working for the right company with juicy stock options proves one's worthiness or unworthiness. Having a great 401-K or smart IRA's certainly prove one's worth and improves one's net-worth.

At Hollywood and Vine the beautiful people gather and would tell us that we not only have to *look* right, we have to *act* right. We have to be intelligent, clever, witty, and have perfect moves. *Then* we can measure up—if we can get an Oscar!

On Pennsylvania Avenue in Washington, DC, we know that having power is the way to worthiness. Being in Congress is great. Being a Senator is better yet. Being president is best of all. *Then* one is worthy—*if* the polls are right and one belongs to the right party. Even then at least 40 percent of the electorate will vote for your opponent and far more than these will never even bother to vote. They neither love your nor hate you—perhaps worse—they don't care!

The sports world is a world of worth. Millions of dollars confirm or deny one's worthiness. Where do you or your children stand in the sport-world worthiness quotient? Are they wearing the right shoes? Do they have the right kind of sunglasses? Do their shirts proclaim winning teams? This is important you know.

Try hard enough, you see, and we don't even need God. Try hard enough and money, fame and fortune will fall our way. Come to think of it, only desperation brings a need for God—except for those few fortunate beings who understand that we can *never* measure up on our own and that the best we can do is God's grace.

Evangelist Billy Graham always concluded his rallies with a hymn that opens the supplicant to God's grace: "Just as I am, without one plea...O Lamb of God, I come, I come." God's grace accepts us as we are and proclaims us worthy. We cannot even hear that proclamation if our hands are full of our own trying to measure up. Only empty hands can receive the bounty of God's worth-fullness.

Worship gets its name from *worth-ship*. True worship of God proclaims that God alone is worthy and I am worthy only by the grace of God. But how commendable am I by God's grace? TOTALLY! In that amazing grace I am loved and received as God's precious, called, dear son or daughter.

Such grace takes the next element in this prayerful life: Commitment. The posture of COMMITMENT is the posture of hand holding hand—arms linked in common cause. Commitment extends beyond the self to others. Commitment extends beyond the self to a larger cause. Commitment is the willful determination to do something significant; to live life on purpose. Notice the empty hands are no longer empty?

But many today are not ready to commit! In fact there is a pervasive fear of commitment. People are afraid to COMMIT. Couples are afraid to marry because commitment scares them. Since recorded history has kept track of such things, there has never been a time of fewer and later marriages. "Til death do us part" scares people. "It sounds so final," one bride told me a week before her wedding. People fear commitment will limit their freedoms. We are afraid to commit ourselves to any larger project or purpose because we fear failure and limitation of freedom. As time is measured by megahertz, sound bites, and thirty-second commercials, longer term commitments seem unreasonable. The world we occupy is a world of immense change. Today a year is enough time for total obsolescence.

Yet without commitment, life loses something immense, magic, wondrous. An anonymous author, caught that truth when he wrote:

> Until one is committed, there is hesitancy, the chance to draw back, always ineffectiveness. Concerning all acts of initiative (and creation) there is one elementary truth, the ignorance of which kills countless ideas and splendid plans: That the moment one definitely commits oneself, then Providence moves too. All sorts of things occur to help one that would never otherwise have occurred. A whole stream of events issues from the decision, raising in one's favor all manner of unforeseen incidents and meetings and material assistance, which no man could have dreamed would have come his way. I have learned a deep respect for one of Goethe's couplet's:
> *"Whatever you can do, or dream you can, begin it.*
> *Boldness has genius, power and magic in it."*[10]

The grace-filled life of prayer is a life of commitment—to God, to faith, to hope, to love. Taking the "leap of faith" as Kiekegaard called it is exactly that—a leap. It is an uncertain leap that may or may not be true. No one can prove God. No one can prove that we have reason for hope. No one can positively prove that the prayerful life of grace is anything but wishful thinking and delusion.

Even though we cannot see God and usually God's voice is muffled by our activity and noise, the commitment to a power greater than ourselves is a commitment that adds texture and richness to life. No—it does more than that—it provides life with an inner radiance, a supernatural glow from within. Commitment is not an addition or a burden—it is a multiplication of life leading to fullness and satisfaction.

The prayerful life of grace demands throwing ourselves into the arms of the One who made it all. It demands that we trust that which cannot be seen, heard or touched. And the results of such commitment? Ah—that brings us to the best part of all.

The last part of the grace-filled life is the first part of what Paul says to the Philippians: "Rejoice in the Lord always. Again I will say, rejoice." The posture of joy is arms raised overhead in joyful exultation.

I call this portion: _E_njoy. (We could as easily use words such as _E_xuberance or _E_xaltation.) Common vernacular doesn't use the word "rejoice" anymore. The word "joy" is mostly limited to hymns and Christmas cards. But we know what ENJOY means. ENJOY is built upon the beautiful concept of JOY.

Joy is a gift infusing the life that knows grace. As Mother Theresa says,

> Joy is prayer. Joy is strength. Joy is love. The best way to show my gratitude to God is to accept everything, even my problems, with joy. Never let anything so fill you with sorrow as to make you forget for one moment the joy of Christ risen.

Richard Wagner puts it this way, "Joy is not in things: It is in us."

Joy is the consequence of the GRACE-filled, GRACE-full life.

*   *   *

This little book is about grace. Grace is a grand idea, a spiritual ideal, and an attribute of God. As such it can easily elude us. I believe God has made grace real if we but make it real. My desire is to make grace real by connecting it to the palpable and physical earthly vehicle we are all privileged (and condemned) to use—our body. Therefore this book is about the Prayerful POSTURES of Grace.

Notice those postures of grace and prayer. First, hands folded in gratitude. From deep within swells the thankful heart. Then the fingers unfold and palms are upraised in a gesture of release as we let go of our expectations, relationships, and things and our life is exposed in its defenseless nakedness. The unfolded hands cross over the heart as the receiving spirit accepts life on its own terms and especially accepts God's grace. Our own hands embrace the body as God would hug us and accept us as we are. Then our hands extend beyond the self to others and to a cause that is larger than the package of self as we join hands with others and willfully dedicate ourselves to a larger purpose. Finally hands joyously upraised express the exuberant soul of union with God and the universe.

In ever-growing circles, the prayerful postures of grace starts deep within with gratitude and grows in concentric circles of open-handed release, crossed arm acceptance, linked arm commitment, and upraised arms of exuberance. As a pebble creates waves on the placid pond, so the prayerful life of grace extends to a life that is significant—making a mark on God's pond of life.

This week, when life starts chipping away at your vitality, just remember GRACE: Gratitude, Release, Acceptance, Commitment, and Enjoyment. Find your joy in the God who enjoys you.

CHAPTER TWO

▼

GRACIOUS GRATITUDE (The Posture of Praying Hands)

Grace to you and peace from God our Father and the Lord Jesus Christ. I give thanks to my God always for you because of the grace of God that has been given you in Christ Jesus... (1 Corinthians 1:3-4)

The first word of <u>GRACE</u> is <u>Gratitude.</u>

When I was a boy, my sister and I would delight when someone had eaten the breast of chicken. The delight in that part of a chicken lay in the wishbone. After eating the meat from the breast we were eager to break the wishbone. We would each take a side of the wishbone, pause for a moment to think of a wish. Usually, in the middle of my thought, before I knew what was happening, the bone was broken and my sister ALWAYS had the "wish" side—the side that, in children's minds at least, granted the holder of that part of the bone his or her wish. It didn't take much digging to learn my sister's secret. She got the larger portion of the wishbone because she put her thumb against the middle portion of the bone assuring her more leverage. And she did it so rapidly that the bone was broken before I caught her at this deception.

"No fair," I would say. "Prove it," she would reply. And I was faced with the dilemma of proving that one cannot put one's thumb against the middle portion of the wishbone. Where, exactly, does one receive confirmation that cheating in this manner in any way negates the effects of one's wish? Where does it say those breaking the wishbone have to break it simultaneously? So—I never knew if her methods were valid or not. But I knew she always got the wish side of the bone and I didn't.

THE DARK SIDE

Wishing is an important part of life. As we go through life, we have many wishes. All of us wish the best for ourselves—good health, good looks, possessions and the means to do what we want. We want a good name. We want to be loved and respected. We all want these goods. I don't know anyone not wanting the best that life can offer for him or herself. If life were a wishbone, we would all want the larger piece.

But life (like my sister) is not fair. Things happen that minimizes the abundant good and diverts our attention to what seems lacking. By seeing what we don't have, how can anyone be happy? How can the fullness of life come to us when our glass is half empty?

The first ingredient in living the grace-filled, prayerful life is gratitude for what we have. Unlike my resentfulness at my sister's having the larger portion of the wishbone, gratitude teaches us to focus on that which is important.

Gratitude looks at the glass as at least half full. Meister Eckhart, Medieval theologian said, "If the only prayer you ever say in your entire life is thank you, it will be enough." Ah—yes!

A young boy and his doting grandmother were walking along the seashore when a huge wave appeared out of nowhere, sweeping the child out to sea. The horrified woman fell to her knees, raised her eyes to the heavens and begged the Lord to return her beloved grandson. Then, miraculously, another wave reared up and deposited the stunned child on the sand before her. The grandmother looked the boy over carefully. He was fine. But still she stared up angrily toward the heavens. "When we came," she snapped indignantly, "he had a hat! And he was dry!"

Gratitude and grace have the same root: GRATIA, which comes from the Latin and means "out of kindness". If we receive something today GRATIS, that means we obtain it freely, without charge. Just like grace. The response to this free gift is GRATITUDE. GRACE and GRATI-TUDE have the same origin in our language because they are so closely linked. A wise one has said, "No gift is truly ours until we have thanked the giver." The response of thankfulness completes the giving transaction.

> Two men look out through the same bars;
> One sees mud, and one the stars.[11]

Gratitude is an option that is based on nothing but attitude. Some multi-billionaires lack an ounce of appreciation whereas some third-world people who do not know whether there will be a next meal have tons of gratefulness. Gratitude is not based on external circumstances. Like grace, gratitude is based solely on the internal perception of life's goodness. Gratitude is an attitude thing. Our favorite attitude should be gratitude.

There is always something for which to be thankful. If you cannot be content with what you have received, be thankful for what you have escaped. If you cannot experience life without pain, then relish the painless moments. As someone has humorously put it: even if you cannot pay your bills, you can at least be thankful you are not one of your creditors. There is always something for which a person can be thankful.

Pity the person whose heart is filled with gratitude and has no one to thank. An atheist cannot thank God for the beautiful sunrise. He cannot thank God for the pleasure of food. She cannot thank God for the joys of everyday life and living. For gratitude to be complete, there has to be a response. Gratitude and faith are so close! Grace and gratitude are intimately tied together.

The natural posture of gratitude is the posture of hands clasped in prayer. It is only natural for a person to turn to God when hearts overflow with gratitude. The traditional posture of prayer becomes the first posture of GRACE: clasped hands with fingers embracing fingers in a warm fold about the size of the human heart which spatially and figuratively are not too distant.

The Apostle Paul illustrates the principle of thanking God even when the external circumstances are less than perfect. His letter to the Philippians was composed in prison. Bear in mind, prisons in Paul's day were primitive beyond most of our imagining, never-the-less, Paul says to the Philippians, "I have learned to be content with whatever I have. I know what it is to have little, and I know what it is to have plenty. In any and all circumstances I have learned the secret of being well-fed and of going hungry, of having plenty and of being in need. I can do all things through him who strengthens me."[12]

In 1621, when Elder Brewster suggested that beginning Tuesday and continuing through Saturday there would be a festival of Thanksgiving, it must have caught some by surprise because it had been a ghastly time for the settlers. Half of those who came died that first winter. Graves were made flat so the Native Americans, in case they were not friendly, would not know how many of their number had died. But still there was much for which to be thankful.

Something of that same attitude attended the official proclamation of a National Fast Day. The nation had endured its darkest hour in the Civil War. Blood flowed freely and brother rose against brother and never before or since has this nation suffered such a calamitous time. Yet President Abraham Lincoln, on October 3, 1863 proclaimed the last Thursday of November 1863 as a national Thanksgiving Day, not for a specific Union victory or event, but a simple time to be thankful for all the year's blessings:

> The year that is drawing towards its close has been filled with the blessings of fruitful fields and healthful skies. To these bounties, which are so constantly enjoyed that we are prone to forget the source from which they come, others have been added, which are of so extraordinary a nature, that they cannot fail to penetrate and soften even the heart which is habitually insensible to the ever watchful providence of Almighty God.

> In the midst of a civil war of unequalled magnitude and severity, which has sometimes seemed to foreign States to invite and to provoke their aggression, peace has been preserved with all nations, order has been maintained, the laws have been respected and obeyed, and harmony has prevailed everywhere except in the theatre of military conflict; while that theatre has been greatly contracted by the advancing armies and navies of the Union.

Needful diversions of wealth and of strength from the fields of peaceful industry to the national defense have not arrested the plough, the shuttle or the ship; the axe has enlarged the borders of our settlements, and the mines, as well of iron and coal as of the precious metals, have yielded even more abundantly than heretofore.

Population has steadily increased, notwithstanding the waste that has been made in the camp, the siege and the battlefield; and the country, rejoicing in the consciousness of augmented strength and vigor, is permitted to expect continuance of years with large increase of freedom.

No human counsel hath devised nor hath any mortal hand worked out these great things. They are the gracious gifts of the Most High God, who, while dealing with us in anger for our sins, hath nevertheless remembered mercy. It has seemed to me fit and proper that they should be solemnly, reverently and gratefully acknowledged as with one heart and one voice by the whole American People. I do therefore invite my fellow citizens in every part of the United States, and also those who are at sea and those who are sojourning in foreign lands, to set apart and observe the last Thursday of November next, as a day of Thanksgiving and Praise to our beneficent Father who dwelleth in the Heavens…[13]

Since then Thanksgiving Day has become a national holiday.

Every year the federal government prints office calendars for the upcoming year. In 1972, someone made a colossal mistake on the calendars for 1973. The mistake assigned November 29th as the holiday. That was not correct. It should have been when it always is—by presidential proclamation—the fourth Thursday in November. In 1973 that would have been November 22nd and not the 29th as the calendar stated.

Rather than destroy the one million calendars that had already been printed, the General Services Administration decided to simply attach a correction to each of the calendars and let it go at that. Here is what the correction said: "Please excuse, but we're giving thanks on the wrong day this year. It's November 22nd"

I once had a Thanksgiving sermon where I proposed that Thanksgiving Day be set aside as the ONE DAY WE DON'T GIVE THANKS instead of the one in which we do! Think of the implications. Instead of setting aside one day a year to give thanks (and indeed many [perhaps most?] people don't use Thanksgiving Day for genuine gratitude), you set aside just one day were one deliberately does NOT give thanks. That might draw more attention to what the prayerful, grace-full life is all about. Indeed, it seems that many have found Thanksgiving Day *not* to be a day of thanksgiving and prayer. Instead, for many, Thanksgiving Day has become "Turkey Day" and the prevailing custom is that we gather with as many family and friends we can corral to watch televised football games and eat. Lincoln proclaimed a national day of fasting (doing without food) and we have turned it into a day of gluttony.

The component of giving thanks seems foreign to most Americans. Perhaps people have lost contact and awareness of the One to whom they can give thanks.

During the week of Thanksgiving, many Christians gather in worship services to give thanks. One hymn has emerged as a favorite: "Now Thank We All Our God" by Martin Rinkart:

> Now thank we all our God
> With hearts and hands and voices,
> Who wondrous things has done,
> In whom his world rejoices;

Who, from our mothers' arms,
Has blest us on our way
With countless gifts of love,
And still is ours today.[14]

Hearing and singing these exalted words, one would never realize that this paean of thanks and praise was composed during times of some of the most severe of human hardships—an awful time of poverty, loss and war. Martin Rinkart was pastor in the town of Eilenberg in Germany, beginning his pastorate near the outset of the Thirty Years' War. Since Eilenberg was a walled city, people from miles around sought refuge there, and overcrowding resulted in extreme poverty and disease. In 1637 the two remaining clergymen died and Rinkart alone was left to minister to the city. It is said that sometimes he preached burial services for forty or fifty people a day. His own wife was taken by the pestilence, and he himself fell ill, but survived. He negotiated with the commander seeking to avert excessive tributes against the impoverished town. And his reward for all his labor? Harassment by the authorities.

Despite it all, he could compose and sing a song of praise to God. If he could do it and the Pilgrims and Abraham Lincoln and Paul could do it, surely there is something in this very moment for which each of us can find reason for thanks.

THE BRIGHT SIDE

Every day God gifts us with a rising sun. Every day God gifts us with energy to live and move and have our being. Every day God gifts us with time and God gifts us with ourselves. We may not all experience the joy of love or the wonder of wealth. We may not all possess the verve of health or the fortune of pain-free mobility. But every day and in every moment,

God's grace is at work. I love the way Henri Nouwen put it: "Everything is, is freely given by the God of love. All is grace. Light and water, shelter and food, work and free time, children, parents, grandparents, life and death— it is all given to us. Why? So that we can say thanks; thanks to God, thanks to each other, thanks to all and everyone."

For the Christian, the chief reason for thanks is found in Paul's letter to the Philippians: "The Lord is near."[15] Our God is not in some remote corner of the universe. No! Our God is in the moment. Our God is in the pain. Our God is in the loneliness. Our God is a present God. No one and no circumstance can take that fact away. Most especially death cannot take the fact of God's nearness from the believer. For as Paul reminds us, "The Lord is near."

How well I remember the first funeral I conducted as a young pastor. I felt so inadequate for the job and the widow wept in such a heart-wrenching manner because she was not at her beloved's side when he breathed his last. "He died all alone," she wailed. My sermon text at the funeral was from Paul: "Who will separate us from the love of Christ? Will hardship, or distress, or persecution, or famine, or nakedness, or peril, or sword?… No, in all these things we are more than conquerors through him who loved us. For I am convinced that neither death, nor life, nor angels, nor rulers, nor things present, nor things to come, nor powers, nor height, nor depth, nor anything else in all creation, will be able to separate us from the love of God in Christ Jesus our Lord."[16]

In my own awkwardness I sputtered what was probably the best that could have been mouthed: "He was not alone when he died," I said. "Jesus was with him." And he was!

For you and for me, the one thing we can believe is that "the Lord is near." And if that is so, then we have reason to give thanks to God. Though everything in the world go wrong for us; though pain rack our bodies or guilt prick our consciences, "the Lord is near" and that is enough. We can breathe a breath of "THANKS BE TO GOD."

A popular reproduction of a set of paintings that grace many homes features an elderly man and another of an elderly woman—each bowed with hands clasped over their dinner tables. The prayerful, gracious life is a life of folded hands. It is a life of prayer—"saying grace." And the root of that prayer is the natural inclination to give thanks to God. Life lived in grace is a life lived in gratitude. The two are as close to one-another as breath and life.

A beloved grandfather explained to his grandson the tradition of breaking the wishbone. At the Thanksgiving dinner, the grandfather and his grandson broke the bone and, unfortunately, the grandson came up with the small end of the bone. Grandfather saw the disappointment in his face and, with a hug said, "That's okay son. *My* wish was that you would get *your* wish."

We have a God who wants the best for us: life in all its fullness. That was why he sent Jesus. The best we can have is a prayerful life of grace. That prayerful life begins when we know how to be thankful for what we have and can ignore what we do not have. The best and fullest life is the happy, grace-filled, prayerful life lived in thankfulness and gratitude for all that we have received—especially for the grace of a God whose one wish is that we get ours. May God bless you with the joy that inevitably follows sincere gratitude.

CHAPTER THREE

▼

RELEASE & RECEIVE (THE POSTURE OF OPEN HANDS)

The spirit of the Lord GOD is upon me, because the LORD has anointed me; he has sent me to bring good news to the oppressed, to bind up the brokenhearted, to proclaim liberty to the captives, and release to the prisoners; to proclaim the year of the Lord's favor, and the day of vengeance of our God; to comfort all who mourn; to provide for those who mourn in Zion—to give them a garland instead of ashes, the oil of gladness instead of mourning, the mantle of praise instead of a faint spirit. (Isaiah 61:1-3)

Demosthenes, the great Greek orator had tremendous popularity as a public speaker, but few appreciated his political views.

On one occasion Demosthenes could not even speak because of the heckling crowd. So he stopped. "I'd like to tell you a story," he said. The audience hushed in anticipation of the verbal gems they would receive.

"A young man leased an ass for the journey to his home," Demosthenes began. "But it was summertime and very hot. Both the owner of the ass and the young man leasing the animal wanted to sit in the shade of it. The owner said he leased the ass for travel not for shade. The young man said the opposite—that he leased the animal for shade and not for travel."

With this much of the story told, Demosthenes dismounted the podium. The Athenians wanted to hear the rest of the story. "Why do you want to hear the end of the story of an ass's shade when you will not listen to matters of great importance?" he asked the audience.

Even more than Demosthenes, God has a wonderful, important story to tell. But we are so occupied and our hands are so full that we cannot receive the great gift of God, grace. We can only handle the many small gifts of our things, our immediate thoughts, and our nearest relationships.

The prayerful life of grace begins with G, representing GRATITUDE. The prayer stance of a person with GRATITUDE is clasped hands. The clasped hands posture is probably the posture most people think of when they think of prayer. But the Bible often speaks of another way to pray—with hands wide open—in a releasing posture. To receive, hands must be empty. The R of *GRACE* is *Release*.

That greatly beloved hymn, "Rock of Ages" has a stanza that says,

> Nothing in my hands I bring; Simply to thy cross I cling.
> Naked, come to thee for dress; Helpless look to thee for grace;[17]

Jesus portrayed empty, open hands, when he taught his disciples to pray, "Thy will be done..." Praying for God's will to be done means releasing life's circumstances to God and opting for a larger life—the life of the kingdom of God. That life is larger than this little earth and greater than the short span of years any of us is privileged to live.

The very heart of prayer comes when we can "let go and let God." Releasing everything to God is central to the prayerful life of grace.

George MacDonald writes, "Man finds it hard to get what he wants, because he does not want the best; God finds it hard to give, because He would give the best, and man will not take it."[18]

The Bible speaks about the great sin of our trying to be gods unto ourselves instead of trusting God. The Genesis story, the first commandment, and Jesus' parables speak of letting God be God. But we would rather grab and hold on and control. We don't want to move over for another God—a *higher power* (than self). We like being God. We like being in control. We like having things go our way. We like being in the very center.

God has created us with more control than any creature in our world. In the very first chapter of the Bible we read, "God blessed them (Adam and Eve), and God said to them, 'Be fruitful and multiply, and fill the earth and subdue it; and have dominion over the fish of the sea and over the birds of the air and over every living thing that moves upon the earth.'"[19] Throughout much of human life we must be in control and take responsibility for our lives, the lives of others dependent upon us, and the stewardship of our jobs and the earth itself.

But too easily we lose perspective and assume too much control. We forget that we are not in control of everything. We forget that one important fact that we are not God. The result is that we bring peril to ourselves and those who know and love us. The "Serenity Prayer" mentioned in Chapter One by Reinhold Niebuhr puts things in perspective:

> God, grant me the serenity to accept the things I cannot change;
> Courage to change the things I can; and
> Wisdom to know the difference.

We could perhaps further refine this prayer to say, "God, grant me the serenity to accept the things I cannot *control...*" The problem, for many of us, comes in those things we bang our heads against a wall trying to control that we have no hope of controlling. I find the rest of Niebuhr's prayer says it well:

> Living one day at a time;
> Enjoying one moment at a time;
> Accepting hardship
> As the pathway to peace.
> Taking, as he did,
> This sinful world as it is,
> Not as I would have it.
> Trusting that he will make
> All things right
> If I surrender to his will
> That I may be reasonably happy
> In this life,
> And supremely happy
> With him forever in the next.[20]

There are so many things to let go of and let God have. Let's look at some of the important things we often try to control that keep us from living a full, prayerful life of grace:

THE DARK SIDE

SIN

Sin is such an old-fashion word and many (perhaps most?) people believe sin is such an outdated concept that it should not be used in normal conversation or thought. Someone has noted, "It says something about our times when you rarely see the word 'sinful' except to describe a really good dessert."

Having no clear understanding or common definition of sin is part of the problem. To some sin is disobeying the commandments of God. Others see sin as going against conscience. The root definition of sin comes from the premise that God is a God of grace and therefore does not desire or take pleasure in seeing any of his creation hurt. If we sin, we hurt—ourselves, others, the created order—whatever. Sin tears down those precious ones God loves. Therefore sin is not hurtful because it is forbidden—but is forbidden because it is hurtful. Jesus says the whole sum of God's law is in obedience to the law of love.[21] Sin violates grace.

Conscience is the best detector of sin. One writer puts it this way, "I know what I should do; there is nothing in the teachings of Christ that is clearer: go and love. But knowledge is one thing, deed another. It seems as though I am two persons. One agrees with Christ and issues the appropriate orders. The other, with his own peculiar serenity, plays deaf, and continues to live as though my ego were the central point of the cosmos and all galaxys revolved around it.[22]

Most of us know our areas of fault, defect—yes—sin. Here's the challenge: With open hands, lay your sin before you. If you have not done this before, it is conceivable that just laying one's sins out and letting them go could take a long, long time. Some will spend considerable time coming to grip with the concept of "sin." They will spend an even longer time letting go of sin. Others may do so incrementally each time they come before God.

How much letting go of sin is necessary? I leave the answer to you but perhaps the following little story says enough. It is a story that is perhaps told in countless households across the land with varying versions of the same basic truth.

When four-year-old Noah got a new baby brother, he resented him. As the boys grew, baby brother received merciless torment from his older sibling. Each time the bigger boy took advantage of the younger, he would say to his crying brother, "Please don't cry, Bobby. I'm sorry. I won't do that again."

One day Noah was taking clods of earth and throwing them in the air near where his brother was playing in the yard. One of the clods disintegrated in a cloud of dust over the head of little Bobby causing the boy to cry as he headed for the protective arms of mother. Noah apologized profusely. "This time I really *am* sorry, Bobby. Please don't tell mother. I'll *never* do that again. Please…"

Little Bobby answered, "I know you are sorry, but what I want to know is are you sorry enough to quit teasing me?"

We can let go of sin totally. We can empty ourselves of pent-up sin. We can let it flow through our fingers like sand until not a grain is left within. We'll talk a little more about this when we discuss guilt.

Letting go completely does *not* mean any of us achieves perfection and never acts against grace ever again. I am convinced the most dangerous people alive are those who believe they have achieved righteousness and perfection. The ones who believe they no longer sin scare me. Part of our human nature constantly struggles against grace. As good and wonderful as it is to live in grace, there is a part of our ancient self that will struggle against it so long as we live. As with all letting go, letting go of grace is a process and not a destination.

ANGER

Anger occurs when life or life's situations do not turn out as we ordain. We expect life to be fair and it is not. So our anger emerges. Given enough frustration and the right kind of temperament, anger can consume us. Paul writes to the Ephesians: "Put away from you all bitterness and wrath and anger and wrangling and slander, together with all malice, and be kind to one another, tenderhearted, forgiving one another, as God in Christ has forgiven you."[23]

Anger is an emotion that we often have difficulty dealing with as human beings. We have used anger to justify war, repression, violence and all kinds of evil. The hardest thing for an angry person to do is to take responsibility for the angry feeling. The healthy individual and a fit society take responsibility for anger. As one prominent Lutheran theologian put it, "As a society, we seem to believe that if our behavior is biologically determined, then the genes we inherit—not we ourselves—can be held responsible for what we do. Confronted by moments of moral crises, we are often quick to scapegoat our genes."[24]

Instead of blaming our genes, or the perpetrator or life's circumstances, the best thing we can do with our anger is to release it to God. Let God be judge and put away bitterness, desire for revenge, and all resentment. God can handle our anger and can give us life in return for it.

Some of the most troubling and troublesome anger I have witnessed is anger at God. In this case the object of our anger *is* God. That makes letting go of our anger *to* God particularly difficult. Fortunately grace teaches us that God is bigger than our anger and it is okay to be angry with God as well. Letting go requires no object. If it is helpful to let go of anger *to* God, great. If the anger is *with* God, then letting go into the thin air works just as well. What is important is that *all* anger gets released.

The Gallup Organization conducted an interesting study in 1994 in which they measured the "hostility index" of various U.S. cities. The hostility index was based on a nine-question scale that asked people how they felt about various issues such as loud rock music, supermarket checkout lines, and traffic jams. Those cities scoring highest on the "hostility index" had another interesting correlation: they had the highest death rates!

Commenting on the study, Dr. Redford Williams of Duke University Medical School said, "Anger kills. There is a strong correlation between hostility and death rates. The angrier people are and the more cynical they are, the shorter their life span."[25]

Dr. Robert R. Kopp puts it this way: grudge-holders are grave-diggers and the only graves they dig are their own.[26] How much better everyone is if we can let go of resentment, grudges and anger's other relatives.

Our anger at people arises in the same way it is roused by circumstances— because people, like life's situations, don't act, speak or think as they *should*. Henri Nouwen said, "forgiveness is love practiced by people who love poorly."[27] If we all just loved better, we would not need to be forgiven or to forgive because we would never hurt others by what we do or what we say.

Former President Dwight D. Eisenhower had an interesting way of letting go of anger. He once said, "I make it a practice to avoid hating anyone. If someone's been guilty of despicable actions, especially toward me, I try to forget him. I used to follow a practice—somewhat contrived, I admit—to write the man's name on a piece of scrap paper, drop it into the lowest drawer of my desk. That drawer became over the years a sort of private wastebasket for crumpled-up spite and discarded personalities. Besides, it seemed to be effective, and helped me avoid harboring useless black feelings."[28]

Write the wonderful word *IMPERTURBABLE* on a Post It sheet and stick that sheet wherever you will see it often. You might find it as a bookmark in your diary or on a bathroom mirror. Let that wonderful word sink deep into your subconscious. Let that word describe *you* and let that description work its magic on you as the realization that you truly can be *imperturbable* because you can grow into *imperturbability. (The word "imperturbable" means to be unshakably calm and collected—yes, even when life slings its arrows and flings its stones.)*

Another way to keep anger from destroying you and your relationships, also admittedly contrived, is to open one's hands in a letting-go posture, and consciously release to God people or situations that cause us grief and anger. Thought and action are powerful.

Whole volumes have been written about anger and how to properly deal with it. We have neither the time nor the space to explore anger in depth, but all of us can at least try the simple approach of RELEASE.

GUILT

English essayist William Hazlitt said, "It is well that there is no one without a fault; for he would not have a friend in the world."[29] Everyone is guilty of doing or saying things that hurt self or others. But some people seem to hold on to their guilt as if it were some precious prize. It seems to confirm a deep sense of unworthiness.

There are several ways of dealing with guilt. A person can deny it and insist that it doesn't really bother. I have found that guilt handled in this way tends to eat away at the soul and actually does more harm than "'fessing up" to the imperfection commonly shared by all humanity. Denial just doesn't work.

Another mechanism people have used in dealing with guilt is to work out self-punishment. I once knew of a man who took Jesus' instruction to mutilate oneself for sin literally.[30] This man's guilt was positively overwhelming. So on a cold winter day, he went to his basement and held his offending hand over the flames of his house furnace. It ruined the man's hand and gave him enormous physical pain. All this really did nothing but relieve a guilty conscience—for a time.

So, how does one deal with guilt? Time and human experience teaches us the best way to handle guilt. But the best way is also the least-used way. That way is to confess it and release it. If it is possible, go to the offended party and seek amends, but if that is not possible or if reconciliation is impossible, let go of the guilt!

I came across a story about a man went to see a psychologist. Unlike many people who go to see a psychologist, this man knew what was bothering him. Several years before, he had taken an exam—in a course on the classical Greek language of all things—and he had accidentally omitted one section of the test. He had forgotten to translate one paragraph from Greek to English.

The man had been a good student, so the professor called his home to ask what had happened. When the student said that he was unaware of the omission, the professor offered to accept the translation over the telephone. The student quickly opened his textbook, found the translation, and read it to the professor. As he later explained to his therapist, "I got an A in the class, but to this day I can't look that professor in the eye." He said, "Whenever I think about the test, I feel terrible!"

Some psychologists would take a passive approach to such a confession, but this one did something very different. He told his client to call the professor and admit his guilt. The man responded that he had considered doing that, but he just couldn't. He couldn't face the shame.

But when the man returned for his next appointment, he walked into the psychologist's office with a new spring in his step. He said, "I did it!" He had called the professor. They had a long conversation. He said, "I feel a hundred pounds lighter." He had been imprisoned by his guilt. Having made his confession, he was free.[31]

Confession truly is good for the soul! Letting go of all guilt is a great next step.

Hanging on to guilt does nothing worthwhile. It only destroys the guilty party. What good does any kind of destruction do? The God who created us does not desire our destruction. God would have us live life in all its fullness. Guilt prevents that and makes the fullness of life impossible. Guilt only weighs down the human soul. Release lifts the weight of guilt and grants newness of life.

A SENSE OF UNWORTHINESS

Who deserves the good things of God and creation? None of us asked to be born into this world? None asked for a body, a mind, a soul. None earned the joy of family and friends. None earned the gift of grace itself. All is given.

Life and grace are gifts of God. Life and grace are never matters of worthiness or unworthiness! Yet we make them so.

I came across the following e-mail from a friend and used it in one of my sermons. The source is unknown but the lesson applies:

A well-known speaker began his seminar on self-esteem by holding up a $20 bill. In the room of 200, he asked, "Who would like this $20 bill?" Hands started going up. He said, "I am going to give this $20 to one of you but first, let me do this." He began to crumple the bill. Then he asked, "Now who wants it?" Still the hands waved in the air. "Well," he replied, "What if I do this?" And he dropped it on the floor and started to grind it into the carpet with his shoe. He reached down to the carpet retrieving crumpled and dirty bill. "Now who still wants it?"

Still the hands went into the air. "My friends, you have all learned a valuable lesson. No matter what I did to the money, you still wanted it because it did not decrease in value. It is still worth $20. Many times in our lives, we are dropped, crumpled, and ground into the dirt by the decisions we make and the circumstances that come our way. We feel as though we are worthless. But no matter what has happened or what will happen, you will never lose your value in God's eyes. To God, dirty or clean, crumpled or finely creased, you are still priceless.[32]

More than a twenty-dollar bill, you and I are worthy and dare not enter-tain the thought that any reason should suggest otherwise. Let go of any sense of unworthiness. Let all of it go. You need no money, no time, no loved ones to be worthy. You are worthy by virtue of your creation. You *are* and hence you *are worthy*! You must release all feelings of unworthiness in this posture of grace.

As with most of what we are discussing, whole volumes have been written on the concept of worth. Various theories go deep into our personal his-tory to show that the sense of unworthiness comes from childhood trauma. We could undergo years of psychotherapy, but until we can let go of our need to be worthy instead of accepting our worth, all that therapy is for naught.

What is standing in the way of you accepting yourself as a worthy, worth-while person? Let go of whatever it is. Accept your acceptability. Accept your acceptance.

PAIN

Like guilt, none of us is immune to pain. Bodies can hurt, minds can clutch hurtful images, souls can long for fellowship with the eternal. But the best recourse to pain is to release it to God. God can and will receive it.

Americans spend billions of dollars on pain relief. We have expectations that we shouldn't have pain. "Normal" suggests pain-free living. Pain indi-cates injury. Pain points to disease. So the presence of pain seems abnor-mal. Often the person in pain tries to explain it as some sort of punishment from God.

Pain itself is a creation of God. Pain tells us of problems. People affected with Hansen's disease (formerly called leprosy) first notice their problem when they experience numbness instead of pain. So a person with Hansen's will wear an ill-fitting shoe that rubs the foot into a blazing and infected blister and not know it. The lack of awareness of pain creates tremendous abuse and ultimate disintegration and disfigurement to the body.

Pain is our body and mind's defense system. For years I have experienced back problems. It would cause me intense pain and lack of mobility. I went to sports physicians, chiropractors, and physical therapists. Various exercises were prescribed but nothing seemed to work. I tried diverse pain medications. Some would make me feel drowsy and others dry mouth. I tried treating the pain with warm packs and, when that didn't work, cold packs. I was given various charts of exercises that promised to help. I tried them all and they did not get rid of the pain. Nothing seemed to work. Then someone told me that perhaps the pain is my mind's way of dealing with other issues. This came at a time when I was experiencing enormous discomfort in my back and underwent more x-rays and eventually an MRI. The x-rays and MRI showed what they had always shown—no back injury.

I started looking at what was going on inside my mind and realized that my back problem was probably my mind's way of telling me about an underlying fear I hadn't wanted to face. Pain can serve us in such ways. And pain can be above any obvious, evident meaning or purpose.

Most troubling, is the persistent, intense pain suffered by innocent people. Witnessing or experiencing apparently purposeless pain allows no Pollyanna view of God and God's grace. Why on earth would a merciful God of grace allow supposed loved ones such pain? Why?

It would be so much easier to believe in God and affirm this wonderful doctrine of grace *if only* there were an explanation to the holocaust or to the apparently meaningless, purposeless tribulations of a good human being. How *does* one explain the deaths of the innocent victims of 9/11? In fact faith and religion seem to answer for most people about any question but in the face of pain, the *why* question serves as a huge stumbling stone on what, for many, is an otherwise smooth highway.

As one writer says, "It would be a great thing to understand pain in all its meanings." But we don't. It is the great mystery. It is the great stumbling stone to faith. It seems to contradict God's love and grace. The only comfort (and it is a slight comfort to those witnessing or experiencing chronic or intense pain) is that pain does seem to affirm the soul's freedom in a universe of choices.

Tim Hansel, a person who himself has suffered tremendous pain frequently uses the expression, "Pain is inevitable, but misery is optional." Pain, like everything else, can be an attitude thing. We can cling to our pain and wear it like Olympic gold. We can rant and rail against it and God's unfair universe. We can condemn ourselves and see our pain as divine punishment of some past sin or the sin of our forebears. Or—we can accept pain and its mystery. We can let go of the pain. We can release it to God. And can choose to live despite the pain. Pain has its options and the option to release it to God is a real one.

The great Christian writer, C. S. Lewis says that pain may be God's way of speaking to us. He says we can ignore pleasure, but pain insists upon attention. "God whispers to us in our pleasures, speaks in our conscience, but shouts in our pains: it is His megaphone to rouse a deaf world."[33] Indeed the fact that Jesus chose to go the way of the cross speaks to the world in a way and with an effectiveness that no pleasure could. The cross reminds us of life as it is and of grace that speaks of God's love.

With open hands we can choose to release the pain to God. If you feel angry with God for the pain, then release the pain to the air. Release requires no object (although I believe having an object makes release easier.) We may not understand the message of our backache (if there is one) and we will not like the discomfort and wish we could dispose of it. But releasing pain to God paves the way for God's grace to shout above whatever bodily, mental, emotional, or spiritual anguish that may lie within our being.

The greatest faith available to human beings is to release that which is incomprehensible and mysterious and beyond present understanding. Pain fits every description. Release that very pain until the faith comes. You will know it. Then you will be free—free to move to the next level of grace and free to move above the pain.

THE APPETITES

We human beings are body, mind and soul. We are one entity. We are one unit. The parts cannot be separated. If the body hurts, it affects our thinking abilities. If the soul is despairing, the effects are shown in the body. If the mind dwells on a subject, that subject will gradually gain dominance in our lives. We are a seamless unit.

Letting go of our bodily appetites is also part of letting go. The hunger for food, for example, can divert our attention—especially if the hunger is great. The longing for sexual gratification can often intrude on our thoughts—especially in times of silence. The emotional insecurities that often form our daily existence can encroach upon our spirituality and keep the soul from any satisfaction.

Prior to engaging in the letting go, open hands posture, make sure you have no physical distractions for they, too, must be released. The best time to release them is when they are not demanding attention. If you are trying to release and the room is bitterly cold, it is going to be difficult to get beyond the body's desire for comfort. If your stomach is demanding attention or your ear attuned to the television quiz show, then release becomes more difficult. It is important that our appetites also receive release. Often they are best released when they are not present or pressing in the moment.

FEAR

Fear and fullness of living are mutually exclusive. Fear can drown the grace of God. The person who is afraid cannot live life fully and cannot experience the fullness of God's rich grace.

Some years ago a well-known television circus show developed a Bengal tiger act, which, like the rest of the show, was done "live" before a large audience. One evening, the tiger trainer went into the cage with several tigers to do a routine performance. The door was locked behind him. The spotlights highlighted the cage, the television cameras moved in close, and the audience watched in suspense as the trainer skillfully put the big cats through their paces. In the middle of the performance, the worst possible fate befell the act: the lights went out! For twenty or thirty long, dark seconds the trainer was locked in with the tigers. In the darkness they could see him, but he could not see them. A whip and a small kitchen chair seemed meager protection under the circumstances, but he survived, and when the lights came on, he calmly finished the performance.

In an interview afterward, the trainer was asked how he felt knowing that the tigers could see him but that he could not see them. He first admitted the chilling fear of the situation, but pointed out that the tigers did not know that he could not see them. He said, "I just kept cracking my whip and talking to them until the lights came on. And they never knew I could not see them as well as they could see me."

We all face tigers in the dark. There are situations that threaten to consume us. Perhaps it is a loved one living a life that poses great threat and danger. Maybe it is a dark secret you harbor that threatens to get loose to embarrass and destroy. Maybe your fear is illness or death. Even people of great faith often have fear when they are dying—not necessarily because they fear death, but because they fear the unknown. Fear is real, but the prayerful life of grace can help us let go of all fear, knowing that God has a view of the end of the story and no fear can overcome God's great story. For the story is HIS-STORY.

No fear or worry can possibly destroy the person living prayerfully. That is a promise of God.

As a minister, I have often had to relate deeply to people who are dying. They know it and their families know it. Dying means releasing everything. There is nothing the dying person can take with him or her in death. All the possessions one has owned will become someone else's. All the joy of good food and restful sleep will pass. The days we so take for granted are coming to an end. The body we lived in all our lives must now be released to the elements from which it came. All the love of family and friends is passing. Nothing represents release more completely than dying! That is what makes dying so tough.

As someone who cares for dying people, I have learned that I myself must make friends with death. The best way for me to make friends with death is to die myself. While I cannot do that literally, I can do it devotionally by releasing to God all that I have received. In the prayerful life of grace, I can let go of everything and cling to God's abundant grace. By doing that myself, I can be an aid and a comfort to those who are forced into doing the same thing by the ending of life.

Fear has no ultimate power when it encounters grace.

Someone has wisely has written,

> Too often fear rules our lives, intruding into every situation. Fear would sit by our sides and whisper gratuitous advice while we make decisions. Fear would embrace us when we meet grief. Fear would seize our sleeves when we step forward. Fear would fray our bodies and our minds, and rob us of the very sleep we need to mend them.
>
> Fear masquerades in countless forms and under many names: Doubt, Indecision, Procrastination, Alarm, Timidity, Anxiety. In dress clothes Fear becomes Terror, Horror, Shock, Consternation.
>
> Fear constantly knocks at our door, asking to enter our lives. Fear poses as a friend. Fear claims to be Prudence, Caution, Care, Diligence, and Discretion. But if we open the house of our lives to Fear, we admit a guest who will not soon or gracefully depart.
>
> FAITH is the comrade who will serve us best against Fear. For Fear is shadow, but Faith is real. Faith, too, assumes other shames and names. There is the faith that is met as Prayer, the alliance with the Almighty that enables one to meet the contrary ways of the world. Faith is the Courage that has battled for man's highest ideals. Some have known Faith as Will-to-live when Fear would bring Death also over the threshold. Faith supports us as

Confidence, in ourselves and in those we serve and those who serve us.

KEEP FAITH as a constant Companion. When Fear knocks at your door, send Faith to answer. Faith carries the light of Truth dissolving the shadow of Fear that would blot out every thought and action.[34]

Fear knocked at the door. Faith answered. No one was there!

So let go of Fear. Most of the time fear is merely <u>F</u>alse <u>E</u>vidence <u>A</u>ppearing <u>R</u>eal. It becomes easier to let go of something when that something is usually not even real. Also—just remember—the tigers don't know you can't see them. And that makes an enormous difference!

THE NEED TO CONTROL

Closely related to fear is our need to control. We like to believe we can trust ourselves. It is harder to believe we can trust others or God or even circumstances.

We cause ourselves so much grief when we feel we must control people, outcomes, even God! Let go; let God. Open your hands to let go of the need to control the outcome. Do you not know that God's vision is greater than our limited vision? Do you not know that God's vision extends into eternity whereas ours can go only to the immediate experience of the present or the memory of things past or imagination of the potential future? Do you not know God's abundant love and grace that is freely given to whoever can let go and receive it?

In some ways our need to control—ourselves, our time, life, and others—is a deeply religious concern based on our understanding of who or what is god. Who or what has ultimate authority in our lives? Is it God or self? When we look to ourselves as the source of ultimate authority, then we practice the surest sense of idolatry (properly spelled *I-dolatry*). God becomes a God of the last resort.

A man ventured into establishing a new internet business. To do this he had to sell most of his possessions (including his home), borrow from every friend willing to loan him money, max out his credit cards and plead with his wife and family for trust and understanding. He had confidence in himself, his family and friends had confidence in him, but things just did not turn out the way they should. The man got deeper in debt with seemingly no hope of recovery.

One day the man's wife quietly opened the door of her husband's office and found him bowed over his desk with hands folded in prayer. "Has it come to this?" she asked.

The man had reached the end of his resources. As they say, "there are no atheists in foxholes," and so neither are there atheists when all human resources have given out. It finally, ultimately comes to this.

Above the famous falls of the Rhine River, at the border between Switzerland and Germany, three men were in a boat that capsized, and all three were caught by the rushing stream of water. They called for help. From the shore, someone threw a rope. One of the three reached for the rope and was pulled to safety. Another, completely confused and in fear of dying, clung to the boat. The third wrapped his arms around himself in abject terror. These two died as they were swept over the falls. Only the one who let go was saved.

All three men had the same opportunity but only one could let go so that he could cling to something that would save him. We too must let go of our need to control. Let God be God. Use the resources God gives you and when you must, let go and let God.

MONEY

Money and the things and opportunities money buys probably reflect the most deeply entrenched need to grasp in our materialistic society. The very sight of money stirs emotions that nothing else stirs in quite the same way. We rejoice when money comes our way and despair when it leaves us. Money is the one commodity we most cling to and are most resistant to releasing. For many in western society, money is the proof of one's value; the measure of one's success; the bedrock of one's future. No wonder it's so hard to let go!

I'll never forget a man named Bob who came to our church to worship. He was youthful-looking, mid-fifties in age. I called on him and found that he had been a member of the church years before. Now he wanted to return. Bob had just been diagnosed with colon cancer. His father had died of that same disease and Bob feared the worst. He was afraid it could happen to him and was most fearful that his recent diagnoses came too late. So, as a precaution, he came to church to try to establish or re-establish a relationship with God and find comfort for his uncertain personal destiny.

I spent many hours with Bob. I found that he had a dream he could not release. He dreamed of retiring and building a log cabin in the woods he owned in Northern Michigan. Bob had achieved his first goal of retiring (actually it was an early retirement because of his cancer) and now he wanted to complete his dream. That dream had been such a large part of

Bob's life for so long that he could not imagine *not* building his dream home.

As his cancer progressed and everyone knew there was no hope of overcoming it, Bob clung to his dream—persisted and refused to let go of it. I have never seen a man suffer as much as Bob. His girlfriend once commented to me, "He looks like Christ on the cross." He did. All because he could not, would not, let go.

As the Bible says, there is "a time to seek, and a time to lose; a time to keep, and a time to throw away."[35] Yes, sometimes there is even a time to let go of one's most precious dreams. Many dreams are intimately connected to money because they revolve around the means to achieve them and that means is usually money.

In one's prayer life, letting go means just that—letting go of everything and releasing it all to God. It means letting go of money and all that money can buy. If you are like most people, this may be one of the most difficult things to truly release. I love the way Meister Eckhart, the thirteenth century German mystic and theologian, put it:

> Some people want to see God with their eyes as they see a cow, and to love Him as they love their cow. They love their cow for the milk and cheese and profit it makes them. This is how it is with people who love God for the sake of outward wealth or inward comfort. They do not rightly love God when they love Him for their own advantage. Indeed, I tell you the truth. Any object you have in your mind, however good, will be a barrier between you and the inmost truth.[36]

Letting go means letting go. It even means letting go of the potential benefit of letting go!

THE BRIGHT SIDE

TENSION

Most of what I have mentioned in this chapter has a side effect—tension and stress. It is nice to know that one can also let go of those things that tighten neck muscles and cause headaches, backaches, and high blood pressure. There is obvious benefit to releasing those things that cause stress and tension. That is why I have put the following in the "Bright Side" column of this chapter (even though all release is "bright" because it is *right*.) Once the primary cause of tension is released, the result is peace, relaxation, and rest.

Sometimes, however, one must focus on the tightened body. If you have dutifully tried letting go of all guilt, sense of unworthiness, pain, fear, need to control, concerns about money and whatever else needs releasing, and you still have tight muscles, then release the body itself.

Start with the toes and imagine they are totally relaxed. Move up the body to the feet, ankles, calves, thighs and so forth. Move all the way up to your head. When you reach your neck, let go of any tension there. Likewise the mouth (sometimes we clinch our teeth and are not even aware of it). The muscles around the eyes get a lot of tension use. Go through your whole body and let the muscles go flaccid. Imagine your body as a large sack of beans. Let it become dead weight.

Letting go—RELEASE—means releasing even the body. Most probably the bodily stresses release automatically as individual concerns are released, but it is good to do a body check and focus even on the individual muscles or joints that become the focus of tension.

As with all letting go, even letting go of bodily tension is not usually easy. It has taken a lifetime to get to this point of learning to stress at those things we seek to hang on to. It stands to reason that it will take more than momentary will power to release the body and let go of all tension and stress that tighten muscles in the legs, back, neck, forehead or wherever else there is tightness.

LOVE

Love is such a wonderful thing and we all need as much of it as we can get. Starting early in life the love a child receives has been proven necessary for life itself. An unloved child will not live long in this world. The more love a child receives, the more healthy that child tends to be. As we mature, love expands from parents to siblings to friends to animals to things. Then comes the day we "fall in love" (which sounds so accidental). If blessed with children, love changes nature and expands once again as it centers on their welfare. We want to hold on to our relationships, and never let them go. Love is too wonderful to release. We love other people and feel they are ours. But no one owns another.

I read a heart-wrenching story about a mother who's two-year old was hit by a car. It was a senseless accident. The mom should have paid closer attention and the driver was way too young to be driving as fast as he drove. And now a beautiful, curly-haired, brown-eyed, pixy lay in the hospital intensive care unit hooked up to every kind of tube in every orifice of her beaten little body.

Hours stretched into days and days into weeks and there seemed to be no improvement. Finally, Mom, in desperation cried out to God, "Dear God, heal my little girl." As clearly as she prayed she heard the voice, "She is not yours, she is mine." That voice from within enabled the girl's mother to change her prayer to "thy will be done."

I wish I could say that God performed a wonderful miracle and the little girl revived and her mom learned a positive lesson on releasing love. However, the little girl died and it was tragic. But Mom, especially in her better moments, can say, "She belongs to God. I do not understand why God took her, but I released her to God that day in the hospital and my soul has been at peace since."

As the poet Kahlil Gibran says,
>Your children are not your children.
>They are the sons and daughters of
>   Life's longing for itself.
>They come through you but not from you,
>And though they are with you yet they belong not to you.[37]

There is risk in love. We must be willing to let go of loved ones and must always live with the conscious fact that precious loved ones can be taken from us or—more hurtful yet—may choose to leave. C. S. Lewis said,

>Love anything and your heart will be wrung and possibly broken. If you want to make sure of keeping it intact you must give it to no one, not even an animal. Wrap it carefully round with hobbies and little luxuries; avoid all entanglements. Lock it up safe in the casket or coffin of your selfishness. But in that casket—safe, dark, motionless, airless—it will change. It will not be broken; it will become unbreakable; impenetrable, irredeemable. To love is to be vulnerable.[38]

In love is a supreme irony: the more we cling to it, the more we crush its tender blossom, the more we can let go of love, the more surely its blossom blooms. As wonderful and beautiful as love is, we must be willing to release it.

The needier a person is, the harder it is to accept the release of that most precious human commodity—love. But if a person desires the strength that comes from a grace-filled life, that is, a life that consists of genuine strength, then even love must be released. The release of love is perhaps the best test of strength because we all need to love and be loved so desperately.

Every day the news reports tragic incidents of people who could not let go of love (at least their conception of "love"). Just yesterday I heard about a fatal shooting in the bucolic little town from which I most recently moved. A father shot and killed his three children and wounded his estranged wife. He could not let go of his dream of the family that should be and accept the reality of his own broken marriage. In a desperate attempt to cling to love, he lashed out in destruction.

We have all experienced people whose lives have been shattered by the loss of loved ones. Surely every loss is tragic and wounds deeply, sometimes mortally. We cannot cling to love and claim loved ones as our possession and we certainly would not choose to lose them. But all of us can daily release them. We can never forget them. We may always love them. But we must daily let go and let God. Let the One who fashioned them in the first place resolve what is best for them. What is best for us is to let the beloved go—release them to God.

HOPE

Our hopes and dreams can become such large parts of our lives that we hold on to them as if they were sacred. Even our most cherished hopes must be released to God. In return we get a life that is filled with prayerful, grace-filled (and hence, real) hope. And this is a hope that will not, cannot disappoint. Long before such hope can come, however, we must let go of other "hope." As Ben Franklin said, "He that lives upon hope will die fasting." Much of what we call "hope" is mere wishful thinking—"I *hope* I can come…" "I *hope* the future is better…" "I *hope* things will improve…"

Martin Luther King, Jr. said, "We must accept finite disappointment, but we must never lose infinite hope." Finite disappointment comes from hopes that never materialized. More commonly, finite disappointment is the hope that materializes but is disappointing, small, lacking in satisfaction.

Dante posts a sign that hangs over hell's entrance, "Abandon hope, all ye who enter here." Clinging to hope sometimes seems to be all we have to keep us alive; to keep us going. We *must* believe that things are going to get better. They simply *must* improve. And so we cling to those hopes as if they were some last thread that would pull us to safety. But such hopes often become finite disappointments that can only drive us to despair.

Letting go of hope—perhaps hope that a relationship will improve or that finances get better or that peace will again reign—allows us to be open to real, heaven-sent hope that comes with grace. Just let go—let go of every hope and wish and fantasy. Let go; let God.

FAITH

Even our doubts and questions can and should be released to God. There is so much we do not—indeed cannot—understand. Who can comprehend the size of an atom or what may lie beyond the end of the universe or what came before the big bang? Who can accept the agonizing death of a child? How can faith survive the holocaust? Who can comprehend the torture of individuals? It may sound trite, but God understands and God knows and God's ways are above our ways. Let them go. Let God be God. If we could figure it all out with our three-pound wonder called the brain, then would God really be God? Much of what is called "faith" is really human rationality or emotion.

It goes like this: "I must prove God. There is a creation. How could there be a creation without a Creator? Therefore, there *must* be a God."

Or—"I feel God must exist. I sense a deeper being. I fear death and desire immortality. Therefore, there *must* be a God."

Sometimes the opposite happens: "There can be no God. I have never seen or experienced God, therefore God *must* not exist."

Perhaps more commonly in post-modern society: "I believe God must exist. I cannot prove his existence and it is difficult to believe. Therefore, I am an agnostic—I neither believer nor disbelieve."

Let go of faith—whatever kind of faith you have. Your faith may be in God, in the ultimate reasonableness of reality, or faith in self. Let it go. Release it. Let go of doubt—whatever kind of doubt you have. Let it go. Release it.

GRACE

God gives us everything: our possessions, our selves, and even our time. None of it, however, is really ours. Everything belongs to God. The challenge is ever so simple; ever so awesome—let go of the ownership of all that is "yours". Let go of the ownership of "your" life. Let go of the ownership of "your" time. Let go and let God and behold the splendor as everything takes on a sacred hue and vibrant peace descends.

The process of letting go even means letting go of God's gift of grace. It means letting go of any pretense of earning grace or of grace given as a reward or favor. Christian writer Philip Yancey says, "Grace means there is nothing I can do to make God love me more, and nothing I can do to make God love me less."[39]

Grace goes totally contrary to the human way of looking at life. In daily experience we know that one gets what one earns. An aphorism that has achieved status as truth says, "There is no free lunch." "Everyone and every thing has a price," is another way of saying the same thing. The one exception to these truths is grace. The unbelievable thing about grace is that there are no strings attached. It is free, undeserved, generous. Hands expecting to earn it cannot. Hearts intent on deserving it do not. Intellect planning to understand it will not. So empty your hands even of grace itself. Open them totally.

The ultimate aim of all prayer is union with God and trust in God's ways, power, and the freedom God gives to let nature take its course—even if that course be incredibly painful and lonely. The prayerful life of grace releases to God final authority. The prayerful life of grace flings itself with empty hands asking only for grace alone.

DIFFICULT QUESTIONS

Perhaps the most difficult object or concept to release is our human need to know WHY? Human beings are purpose driven. We know that every-thing has an explanation. We ask questions: WHO? WHAT? WHEN? WHERE? HOW? But the WHY question is the one that often must goes begging.

Why life? Why the universe? Why my existence? Why so much apparently senseless pain? Why must children suffer? Why must I hurt? Why doesn't God speak to me more clearly?

When we cannot answer the WHY question, we are tempted to dismiss the question and either ignore it or give in to meaninglessness. For example, if we cannot understand why suffering, then we want to say, "there must not be a personal God of mercy or else this wouldn't happen." The presumption is that we know more than God. And if we don't know the answer to our own question, then we assume that the subject of our question (God) does not exist. This puts us firmly in the deity seat of our lives instead of releasing that position to God.

When the Apostle Paul experienced a "thorn in the flesh" (pain, frustration, disability) he prayed three times for release. The response from God was direct: "My grace is sufficient for you."[40] Indeed it is. Grace is enough. Grace is sufficient. Pain can perhaps direct our attention to the One who created us. As C. S. Lewis put it: pain is "God's megaphone" to get our attention.

When we sit quietly with open hands and release to God, then we are ready to RECEIVE.

What do we receive? Don't even think about the benefits of reception. Think only of releasing everything. Every pain as well as all comfort, peace, faith, hope, love and joy. Let go of everything. For in letting go, we are in a position to receive.

A wealthy man and his son loved to collect rare works of art. They had everything in their collection, from Picasso to Raphael. They would often sit together and admire the great works of art.

When the Viet Nam conflict broke out, the son went to war. He was very courageous and died in battle while rescuing another soldier. The father was notified and grieved deeply for his only son.

About a month later, just before Christmas, there was a knock at the door. A young man stood at the door with a large package in his hands. He said, "Sir, you don't know me, but I am the soldier for whom your son gave his life. He saved many lives that day, and he was carrying me to safety when a bullet struck him in the heart and he died instantly. He often talked about you, and your love for art."

The young man held out his package. "I know this isn't much. I'm not really a great artist, but I think your son would have wanted you to have this."

The father opened the package. It was a portrait of his son, painted by the young man. He stared in awe at the way the soldier had captured the personality of his son in the painting. The father was so drawn to the eyes that his own eyes welled up with tears. He thanked the young man and offered to pay him for the picture.

"Oh, no sir, I could never repay what your son did for me. It's a gift."

The father hung the portrait over his mantle. Every time visitors came to his home he took them to see the portrait of his son before he showed them any of the other great works he had collected. The man died a few months later.

There was to be a great auction of his paintings. Many influential people gathered, excited over seeing the great paintings and having an opportunity to purchase one for their collection. On the platform sat the painting of the son.

The auctioneer pounded his gavel. "We will start the bidding with this painting of the son. What's the opening bid for this painting?" There was silence. Then a voice in the back of the room shouted. "We want to see the famous works. Skip this one."

But the auctioneer persisted. "Will someone bid for this painting? Who will start the bidding? $100, $200?" Another voice shouted angrily. "We didn't come to see this, we came to see the Van Goghs, the Rembrandts. Get on with the real bids!"

But still the auctioneer continued. "The son! The son! Who'll take the son?"

Finally, a voice came from the very back of the room. It was the long-time gardener of the man and his son. "I'll give $10 for the painting." Being a poor man, it was all he could afford

"We have $10, who will bid $20?"

"Give it to him for $10. Let's see the masters."

"$10 is the bid, won't someone bid $20?" The crowd was becoming angry. They didn't want the picture of the son. They wanted the more worthy investments for their collections. The auctioneer pounded the gavel.

"Going once, twice, SOLD for $10!" A man sitting on the second row shouted. "Now let's get on with the collection!" The auctioneer laid down his gavel. "I'm sorry, the auction is over."
"What about the paintings?"

"I am sorry. When I was called to conduct this auction, I was told of a secret stipulation in the will. I was not allowed to reveal that stipulation until this time. Only the painting of the son would be auctioned. Whoever bought that painting would inherit the entire estate, including the paintings. The man who took the son gets everything!"

God gave his son 2,000 years ago to die on a cruel cross. Much like the auctioneer, His message today is, "The son, the son, who'll take the son?" Because you see, whoever takes the Son gets everything.[41]

Let go of everything and turn it all over to God. It won't even cost you $10. If you have the son, you have it all. For the Son of God spells GRACE—God's love freely and abundantly given. Let go so you can receive. True wealth is wealth of spirit. True wealth is available to every person who can un-clinch his or her fist and can release FEAR, ANGER, GUILT, PAIN, LOVE, HOPE, FAITH and GRACE itself.

When we can let go; RELEASE, then we are open to RECEIVING the life of prayerful grace. God bless your letting go.

CHAPTER FOUR

▼

ACCEPT & APPLY (The Pretzel Posture)

"Ask, and it will be given you; search, and you will find; knock, and the door will be opened for you. For everyone who asks receives, and everyone who searches finds, and for everyone who knocks, the door will be opened. (Matthew 7:7-8)

With empty hands, empty hearts, empty thoughts, empty souls, we come before the throne of God's grace as one who is "poor in spirit."[42] With this emptiness we are finally free to receive. Now we are open. Now we are liberated from all that would tie us down. Now we're getting to the really good stuff. It's something like Christmas to a child (only better!). Remember the anticipation? Can you feel again the good things to come? The hands are open and the gift is on its way. We began with the posture of folded hands—folded in thankfulness and _G_ratitude to God for GRACE. Then our hands _R_eleased everything to God and became empty so they could _A_ccept. The prayerful postures reflect a new reality to receive the gift of _GRA_CE. The gift actually has two parts: the grace of God and life on its own terms. Let's start with life on its own terms.

THE DARK SIDE

LIFE AS IT IS

Life as it is really doesn't sound like a gift. Life on its own terms sounds more like a curse than gift. Life as it really is begins with the labor of childbirth and the trauma of entering a cold, often indifferent and cruel world. Life as it really is often ends in violence or the deterioration of the body and often the mind, and the pain of sickness or injury and the prospect of being cut off from everything and everyone one has known and loved. Suffering, pain, heartbreak and death are guaranteed elements of everyone's life.

I have encountered a number of people angry at life on its own terms. They believe life should be different; life should be fair; life shouldn't be so painful. Just today I had an older man speak to me about his son. "My son's angry because when his son was born, he lived just fifty-two minutes and died. When my son and his wife asked the preacher if this child went to heaven, the minister said, 'No.' Ever since that time my son has been so angry, he won't darken the door of a church even though this happened twenty-two years ago."

I said to this father, "It sounds to me like your son isn't so much angry at what the minister said or didn't say, but I suspect he's very angry at God for letting his child die at such an early age." The father thought for a moment, had a look of insight on his face and said, "You know, I think you're right."

Life on its own terms is not fair or democratic. People are not created equal. Some have all the talent and good looks. Some have all the money they need. Some have all the "luck" and many others seem to have little or nothing. As country folk say, "If it weren't for bad luck, I'd have no luck at all."

Although Jesus spoke of living life on its own terms, the Gospels report that even he on one occasion had trouble with the dark side—life as it really is.

He knew his mission was the way of the cross. He was on his way to Jerusalem to suffer and die but did he really have to go through with the pain? Mark 14:36 says, "He *(Jesus)* said, *(as he was in the Garden of Gethsemane with his disciples just prior to his arrest and torture)* 'Abba,[43] Father, for you all things are possible; remove this cup *(his description of the upcoming suffering)* from me.'"

Jesus well knew what lay ahead. Foreknowledge alone is torture. Most of us don't have the curse of knowing what lay ahead. We hope for the best and often fear the worst. Jesus knew and we can only imagine how knowing that intense torture was in his immediate future would deeply move him to pray, "remove this cup from me." But Mark's gospel adds, "yet, not what I want, but what you want."[44]

The grace of God was shown in a strange way: the cross. The gold cross necklace people wear so casually and that Christian symbol we put on the tops of churches—that little, insignificant symbol, was nothing insignificant to people who had actually experienced real crucifixions. The Romans knew how to use this instrument of torture and they made all challengers to the power of Rome its victims. The Roman authorities wanted everyone to know the consequences of challenging Rome's power. The crosses of those considered enemies of the state were not private executions hidden behind high walls where the agonizing screams of victims would be heard only by official ears. No, their crosses were put at the crossroads and busy highways so people could have maximum exposure to Rome's awful power.

Since the crucifixion of Christ and the founding of the Christian faith, the cross has always been a major "stumbling stone."[45] Paul writes: "Jews demand signs and Greeks desire wisdom, but we proclaim Christ crucified, a stumbling block to Jews and foolishness to Gentiles…"[46] So it was to Jesus and to his people the Jews and to the sophisticated philosophers, the Greeks. And so it still today. The cross is a strange way to express love and grace! The cross is "life on its own terms" taken to the extreme.

There are many things about God we cannot understand. The great WHY questions remain unanswered. God's ways *are* different from and beyond our ways or our mind's understanding. No human mind can fit the mind of God within its understanding. The cross is God's way of saying, in the most extreme way possible, LET GO…LET GOD. When we can do that, then we are open to receiving.

Likewise, unless you want needless and unnecessary additional pain, everyday life must be lived on its own terms. It must be lived daily and in the present. Too much worrying about the future robs one's living and too much regret over the past steals the abundance of life Christ promised.

Peter McWilliam has crafted a beautiful little story that says it so very well:

> When the Earth was almost complete, God gathered the best and the brightest of God's helpers to make one very important decision. Something needed to be hidden until humanity was mature enough to appreciate it and use it properly.
>
> It was the greatest treasure of humankind, the greatest gift, the greatest blessings: it was humanity's true Self—the Self that was

undeniably and experientially linked to the Source of all creation, a direct connection to God and all of Nature.

But where to hide it? Humans had a peculiar characteristic: if they didn't earn what they got, they didn't much appreciate it, and if they didn't appreciate it, they didn't take very good care of it. Immaturity 101. But when humans appreciated something, they took very good care of it, indeed.

But how does one "earn" a gift? This Self was a gift from God, not something to be earned. It was decided that this gift would be hidden, and humanity's "earning" of it would be the finding of it.

"But where to hide it?" God asked the helpers.

"Let's hide it on the highest mountain," suggested one of God's helpers.

"No," said God; "eventually humanity will climb the highest mountain."

"Then let's hide it in the depths of the ocean," suggested another.

"Humanity will someday plumb the depths of the ocean," said God. "Besides, neither of these hiding places gives all of humanity the same opportunity to find it. The poor and the weak must have the same opportunity as the rich and the strong."

This caused something of a pause.

"*Where* are we allowed to hide it?" asked an astute helper.

"As with most things," answered God, "you can hide it in space and in time."

More thinking in the firmament.

After what seemed an eternity (and it could well have been), one of the helpers finally spoke: "The last space humans would think to look for such a gift would be within themselves."

"Yes," agreed another, "we can hide it within each of them, equally."

"That's the last place they'll look," exclaimed another, enthused about the idea.

"You've found an excellent place to hide it," smiled God, "but *when* should they be able to find it?"

"Four A.M. on Tuesday mornings…"

"…but only if Tuesday falls on a leap year…"

"…and they have to have fasted and prayed for three days and nights before…"

"We're making up rules for life," said God, "not a Ninetendo Samurai Warrior game."

A thoughtful silence again settled upon God's Council.

"If we're going to hide it in the most obvious place—within each of them," said a helper, "why not make the finding of it most possible at the most obvious time—right now."

"Here and now…" considered another. "Yes. That would do it."

"Humans are so seldom where they are when they are," agreed a third. "We'll put the gift in the most obvious place—inside each of them; and we'll place it in the most available possible time—right now, the moment."

"And to make matters even more obscure," smiled one helper, "we'll name the gift, and the time when the gift can be found, by the same name."

"The present," another smiled.

"Yes, the present." There was a consensus in heaven.

"Well done," said God. "Now, let's work on The Commandments. how many do we have so far?'

"Three thousand, eight hundred and seventy-four."

"Do you think we can work on shortening these a bit?"

The truth of this story remains unverified—and certainly our telling of it veered on the fanciful. Yet, from what we've been able to discover about the present, it's *as if* it happened that way.[47]

The cross is a most ingenious way to help us focus on living life in the present and on its own terms. God did not spare Jesus, his own beloved, the greatest of pain and most humiliating of all situations and neither does God spare any of us the pain of living from day to day with life making up the rules. The cross is a great reminder of how to live life on its own terms, how to live the prayerful life of grace.

An ancient posture of prayer is hands over one's chest in the form of a cross. Around 610 A.D. in northern Italy a medieval monk awarded pretzels to children as an incentive for memorizing prayers. The monk shaped the pretzel like the folded arms of children in prayer. The original Latin word for "pretzel" comes from the Latin *pretiole* which means "little gift." The Italian word *bracciatelli* means "small arms." Thus, pretzels were gifts in the shape of small, praying arms.[48]

That pretzel you snacked on has its roots in GIFT (as in grace) and PRAYER (as in "the prayerful postures of grace.") It is also cruciform—reminding the receiver and consumer—of life on its own terms as it was when Jesus went to the cross.

The cross is the ultimate extreme of life as it is (not as we would wish). More ordinarily life lived on its own terms means that the traffic light will be red and stay red longer when you are in a hurry. More ordinarily life on its own terms means that the back aches and time passes and birthdays come and go with increasing velocity. More ordinarily life on its own terms means that there is much over which we have no control. But we can ACCEPT life and the various graces of life on its own terms and thereby live the prayerful life of grace.

I received the following story in an e-mail from a friend. The story is life lived on its own terms taken in its most elemental way. My friend added to the story, "We must always keep our prayers in perspective, praying ultimately for God's will for our lives, not ours."

How sad sometimes that we turn our Almighty Father, provider of all things we need, into a "genie." This story touched my heart reminding me that I need to ask for HIS strength to sustain me through times when they are going differently than I expect or even want. And now, the story…

My son Gilbert was eight years old and had been in Cub Scouts only a short time. During one of his meetings he was handed a sheet of paper, a block of wood and four tires and told to return home and give all to "dad."

That was not an easy task for Gilbert to do. Dad was not receptive to doing things with his son. But Gilbert tried. Dad read the paper and scoffed at the idea of making a pine wood derby car with his young, eager son. The block of wood remained untouched as the weeks passed.

Finally, mom stepped in to see if I could figure this all out. The project began. Having no carpentry skills, I decided it would be best if I simply read the directions and let Gilbert do the work. And he did. I read aloud the measurements, the rules of what we could do and what we couldn't do. Within days his block of wood was turning into a pinewood derby car. A little lopsided, but looking great (at least through the eyes of mom). Gilbert had not seen any of the other kids cars and was feeling pretty proud of his "Blue Lightning," the pride that comes with knowing you did something on your own.

Then the big night came. With his blue pinewood derby in his hand and pride in his heart we headed to the big race. Once there my little one's pride turned to humility. Gilbert's car was obviously the only car made entirely on his own. All the other cars were a father-son partnership, with cool paint jobs and sleek body styles made for speed. A few of the boys giggled as they looked at Gilbert's, lopsided, wobbly, unattractive vehicle. To add to the humility Gilbert was the only boy without a man at his side. A couple of the boys who were from single parent homes at least had an uncle or grandfather by their side. Gilbert had "mom."

As the race began it was done in elimination fashion. You kept racing as long as you were the winner. One by one the cars raced down the finely sanded ramp. Finally it was between Gilbert and the sleekest, fastest looking car there. As the last race was about to begin, my wide-eyed, shy eight year-old ask if they could stop the race for a minute, because he wanted to pray. The race stopped.

Gilbert hit his knees clutching his funny looking block of wood between his hands. With a wrinkled brow he set to converse with his Father. He prayed in earnest for a very long minute and a half. Then he stood, smile on his face and announced, "Okay, I am ready."

As the crowd cheered, a boy named Tommy stood with his father as their car sped down the ramp. Gilbert stood with his Father within his heart and watched his block of wood wobble down the ramp with surprisingly great speed and rushed over the finish line a fraction of a second before Tommy's car.

Gilbert leaped into the air with a loud "Thank you" as the crowd roared in approval. The Scout Master came up to Gilbert with microphone in hand and asked the obvious question, "So you prayed to win, huh, Gilbert?"

To which my young son answered, "Oh, no sir. That wouldn't be fair to ask God to help you beat someone else. I just asked Him to make it so I don't cry when I lose."

Children seem to have wisdom far beyond us. Gilbert didn't ask God to win the race, he didn't ask God to fix the outcome, Gilbert asked God to give him strength in the outcome. When Gilbert first saw the other cars he didn't cry out to God, "No fair, they had a father's help." No, he went to his Father for strength.

Perhaps we spend too much of our prayer time asking God to rig the race, to make us number one, or too much time asking God to remove us from the struggle, when we should be seeking God's strength to get through the struggle. "I can do everything through Him who gives me strength." Philippians 4:13[49]

Gilbert's simple prayer spoke volumes to those present that night. He never doubted that God would indeed answer his request. He didn't pray to win and thus hurt someone else. He prayed simply that God would supply him the grace to lose with dignity; grace to live life and its consequences on its own terms. Gilbert, by his stopping the race to speak to his Father also showed the crowd that he wasn't there without a "dad," but his Father was most definitely there with him. Yes, Gilbert walked away a winner that night, with his Father at his side. And had Gilbert's car come in dead last, he still would have won! Gilbert could live life on its own terms. There is great grace in being able to accept, that is, to receive life as it is—not as we might wish.

A large part of receiving life as it is means accepting self as it is. Somewhere Rabbi Joshua Loth Liebman said,

> Let us...learn how to accept ourselves—accept the truth that we are
> capable in some directions and limited in others, that genius is rare,
> that mediocrity is the portion of almost all of us, but that all of us
> can contribute from the storehouse of our skills to the enrichment
> of our common life. Let us accept our emotional frailties, knowing
> that every person has some phobia lurking within his mind and that
> the normal person is he who is willing to accept life with its limita-
> tions and its opportunities joyfully and courageously.[50]

We can all receive the gift that is life, the present moment, and ourselves.
We can, with empty hands, accept all of life as it is. For some of us that
means accepting life with intense pain. For others that means heartbreak.
For still others, accepting life on its own terms means living below the
community standard of living. Living life as it is and accepting life's outcomes, is a great gift. It is grace as surely as life itself is grace: undeserved,
unasked for, a freely-given gift. And the result is PEACE. Profound, wonderful, unearthly, inexplicable peace. "God, grant me the serenity to
accept the things I cannot change..."

THE BRIGHT SIDE

GOD

By letting go, we are free to accept life as it is and, sometimes life on its
own terms is not pleasant or what we might wish for ourselves or others.
But by letting go, something better emerges.

Many people are forced to let go. The old adage says, "There are no atheists in foxholes." A person in a foxhole has precious few options. As we
bump up against the last of human or natural resources, people often find

that letting go brings them into contact with a Greater Reality. In her book, A WINDOW TO HEAVEN, Diane Komp[51] tells the story of Ann and her husband, who might be called typical boomers. Well-off financially, they had no time for God or anything religious. Busy in their separate endeavors, they grew apart. They stayed together, in part, because they loved their children. Mothers aren't supposed to have favorites, but their youngest son, T.J., was Ann's favorite in many ways.

The family had nothing to do with church, so Ann was surprised when T.J., suddenly said one day, "Mama, I love you more than anything in the world, except God. And I love him a little bit more!" Ann wondered why he would suddenly speak of God, especially with such enthusiasm—but she told T.J. that that was fine.

Two days later, on a bitterly cold day, T.J. crossed a snow-covered creek, fell through the ice and died. Ann's world fell completely fell apart. For a life that had nothing to do with God, Ann remembers saying, "I hate you God!" It seemed she had lost everything.

Then she remembered a Christmas gift that T.J. had bought for her. He had tried to give it to her before Christmas, but she told him to put it away until Christmas. When she got home from visiting where T.J. had died, she hurried upstairs to open the present. Inside she found a beautiful necklace with a cross.

T.J.'s gift of faith changed Ann's life. In her brokenness, she was able to receive more than she had lost—she received the Lord. From that experience Ann sensed Christ calling her to reach out to other parents who had lost children. She discovered that she possessed a healing gift for parents in grief. As she ministered to others, she felt Christ ministering to her. She says, "Helping others helped me." In losing she found.

Ann's husband also became a Christian. In their tragedy, they began bring-
ing their separate lives back together again. They founded a ministry that
has helped more than two hundred families. They call it T.J. Ministries.
T.J., of course, was their beloved son's. But the initials, T.J., also mean
something more. They emphasize how Ann and her husband survived
their tragedy. T.J. means Through Jesus. Ann and her husband found
strength to survive through Jesus.

How many stories end with God? In accepting life on its own terms, we
come to a Greater Reality we often call God.

Malcolm Muggeridge lived a long life apart from God. But in the end he
found peace with his Maker. As he put it: "For it is precisely when every
earthly hope has been explored and found wanting, when every possibility
of help from earthly sources has been sought and is not forth-coming, when
every recourse this world offers, moral as well as material, has been explored
to no effect, when in the shivering cold the last twig has been thrown into
the fire and in the gathering darkness every glimmer of light has finally flick-
ered out: it is then that Christ's hand reaches out sure and firm."[52]

THE GIFT OF GRACE ALONE

The present falls into the empty hands of a prayerful life and fills those
hands and hearts and minds and souls with fullness. Accepting life as it is
on its own terms is a great gift but it is not *the* great gift. Receiving ourselves for who and what we are is also a wondrous gift, but it also is not *the*
great gift. For *the* great gift is *the gift of grace.* The great gift of grace *is*
grace.

Receiving the gift of grace is not to attain the gift. A true gift is not earned,
but given freely by the giver. There are no saintly rungs to climb to attain

God's incredible love. That love simply is. The problem is receiving it. Thelma Hall writes:

> Most of us seem to assume that union with God is attained by laboriously ascending a ladder of virtues, which finally fashion our holiness and make us fit for him. In truth, the reverse is far more accurate: the great saints and mystics have been those who fully accept God's love for them. It is this which makes everything else possible. Our incredulity in the face of God's immense love, and also self-hate or an unyielding sense of guilt, can be formidable obstacles to God's love, and are often subtle and unrecognized forms of pride, in putting our "bad" above his mercy.[53]

And what is grace. Again, only by story can I even begin to explain it. Only by story can I even begin to understand it. As Augustine says of God, so goes grace: "Since it is God we are speaking of, you do not understand it. If you could understand it, it would not be God."[54] Similarly, if you or I truly understood grace—the grace that comes from God—then it would no longer truly be God's grace. This whimsical little story partially tells how it is by grace alone that the ball game of life is won.

> Bill was caught up in the spirit where he and the Lord stood by to observe a baseball game. The Lord's team was playing Satan's team. The Lord's team was at bat, the score was tied zero to zero, and it was the bottom of the 9th inning with two outs.

> They continued to watch as a batter stepped up to the plate whose name was Love. Love swung at the first pitch and hit a single, because Love never fails.

> The next batter was named Faith, who also got a single because Faith works with Love. The next batter up was named Godly

Wisdom. Satan wound up and threw the first pitch; Godly Wisdom looked it over and let it pass, because Godly Wisdom does not swing at Satan's pitches. Ball one. Three more pitches and Godly Wisdom walked, because Godly Wisdom never swings at Satan's throws.

The bases were loaded.

The Lord then turned to Bill and told him He was now going to bring in His star player. Up to the plate stepped Grace. Bill said he sure did not look like much! Satan's whole team relaxed when they saw Grace. Thinking he had won the game, Satan wound up and fired his first pitch. To the shock of everyone, Grace hit the ball harder than anyone had ever seen. But Satan was not worried; his center fielder, the Prince of the air, let very few get by. He went up for the ball, but it went right through his glove, hit him on the head and sent him crashing on the ground; then it continued over the fence for a home run!

The Lord then asked Bill if he knew why Love, Faith, and Godly Wisdom could get on base but could not win the game. Bill answered that he did not know why. The Lord explained, "If your love, faith and wisdom had won the game you would think you had done it by yourself. Love, faith and wisdom will get you on base, but only my grace can get you home.[55]

Accept God's grace alone! Even great religious efforts such as total human love, absolute faith, and incredible wisdom will not get you home. Only grace can win the game of life. Accept the infinite love of God for you. And when you doubt that love, wrap yourself in the prayer posture of the pretzel and *know* God's love. You are worth more than you can ever imagine.

You cannot earn such worth; you can only receive it. Accept it freely. There are no strings attached. It is your gift given by the Great Giver.

How can we know this is true? How can we know that grace is real? How can we know that God loves us perfectly? We know it because God sent his Word. It was a living Word—a person. He came as one of us. He lived as one of us. He taught the futility of trying to earn one's place in heaven. He taught that even the lowly, despised and rejected people are precious in God's sight. He taught with words and actions that conveyed love—perfect love, unconditional love. And then he died in a most tragic way as a good, righteous man, his enemies rigged a mob scene and coerced the Roman authorities to execute him as a great criminal and traitor. He endured enormous pain on the cross and yet he had love for those who viciously mistreated him.

While even scripture says in no uncertain terms, "anyone hung on a tree is under God's curse"[56] that tree, the cross, was once a sign for all of the incredible brutality human beings can have for one another. Once the sign of cursedness it has become the very sign of God's love.

The cross was so totally transformed because the one who died on it was totally changed from an earthly body to a resurrected one. The empty grave was proof of something totally new on the face of the earth: grace. The resurrection appearances of Jesus told the world that something earth-shattering happened in that backwater country tucked in the corner of the mighty Roman empire a long time ago.

The cross is God's ironic sign of grace. As an instrument of torture it has been transformed into the great plus sign of life in all its fullness. As "A" is the center of the word GR*A*CE, so the cross is at the center of the concept of grace. It was through the cross that God communicated to us unconditional love and acceptance. It is through the tragic cost of the cross that we begin to understand the free gift of grace.

And the result is PEACE. Profound, wonderful, unearthly, inexplicable peace—the kind that passes all understanding because it is borne of God. As Paul says, *the peace of God, which surpasses all understanding, will guard your hearts and your minds in Christ Jesus.*[57]

CHAPTER FIVE

▼

COMMIT & COMMUNE (THE POSTURE OF JOINED HANDS)

So with yourselves; since you are eager for spiritual gifts, strive to excel in them for building up the church. (1 Corinthians 14:12)

The C of *GRACE* represents Commitment. However it could stand for Core or Center because what comes from the center is how we live out our lives.

I was eating a peach the other day and of course, found the pit in the center. I have eaten thousands of peaches in my life, but my pensive mood set me thinking about purpose (not something eating peaches necessarily engenders in me). Pits are thrown away as we eat peaches. They are nuisances. But at the center of the peach are incredible possibilities for much more than the few bites of taste on my tongue that the flesh of the peach provides me. In the pit lays the potential for a tree and in the tree lays the possibility of thousands upon thousands of other peaches and pits and therefore trees. The world could be over run by peaches if every pit were to perfectly fulfill its purpose!

We human beings also have a center and that center is the root of incredible greatness that far exceeds the individual. As the peach is ultimately about its center, so we are about our center. But, like many peach pits, people squander their centers and throw them away! Think of it this way—most of the people you will meet today have no idea or concern about their life's center—core—pit.

The Dark Side

What is at the center? Usually: the self. We are born that way. Freud insightfully showed us that a child is truly at the center of his or her universe. Everything revolves around the self. And that is as it should be. Without such self-centeredness, the child could not survive!

Gradually most people learn that there are others in this world as well and that they, too, matter. We call this "maturity." As a person grows, he or she moves from total self-absorption to the reality that there are others in this universe. Even though awareness of others exists, the self is still very much at the center. The question that motivates every person is this one: WHAT'S IN IT FOR ME? The "me" part of the question is central. Immature people, like my peach, with self at the center are the pits! But the world is full of self-centered people who have not yet learned that others count.

I saw on the television show "Sixty Minutes" an interview by Ed Bradley with reputed gangster, Anthony Casso. This man has admittedly participated in thirty-six murders. Yet this hardened criminal's eye teared when he thought of his family. Ed Bradley asked him, "What about the families of those you killed. Did you ever think about them?" To which the mobster replied, "I have no regrets. I didn't know them." The implication: if I don't know them, they don't matter. I am the center of my universe and I am the determiner of who or what is important!

The Brighter Side

Many people move to a deeper maturity level. Some people move well beyond themselves and it is evident that they are not the center of their universe.

Renoir, the French artist, was afflicted with acute rheumatoid arthritis and suffered most of his life with that incurable malady. For many years pain compelled him to paint while sitting in a chair. A friend noticed one day that the artist was forcing himself to paint, through almost blinding pain. "You have painted enough," said the friend. "You are established as one of the top artists of France and Europe. Why must you go on, torturing yourself like this?" Renoir hardly looked up from his canvas as he answered, "The pain passes, but the beauty remains."

For Renoir, the self was no longer at the center of his universe. Now it was art; it was beauty. He could sacrifice himself and the torture of the moment to a higher good: art. His maturity had replaced self as the center of the universe and had placed art there instead.

Similarly famed violinist Fritz Kreisler performed so beautifully at a concert that a woman rushed up to him afterwards and said, "I'd give my life to play as beautifully as you do." To which Kreisler replied, "I did." The self had been subjugated to a higher value: music.

Napoleon had a regiment of soldiers he called his "Old Guard" because of their bravery and dependability. Once he stood before this regiment and asked for a volunteer to undertake a hazardous mission. He warned them that the volunteer would probably lose his life. "I will turn my head," Napoleon said, "and if there is a volunteer he will step forward one pace." When Napoleon turned his head back he saw every man in line, no one stood out of the ranks. The emperor was disappointed, but considering the extreme risk involved, he should not have been surprised. An officer, catching his emperor's disappointment, quickly saluted and said, "Sir, every man stepped forward one pace."

These men had different centers. Their highest value was not the self. Their center was patriotism and the emperor. (Although I would suspect some degree of group pressure at play here as well.)

People who have self at the center can only make *contributions* to the greater good. Those who have matured so that something else or someone else is at the center have *commitment* to that greater good.

A corny joke tells about a chicken and a pig who were traveling together and found a place to rest for the evening, but when they arose in the morning, they were both hungry. "Let's find a restaurant for breakfast," the pig suggested. As they traveled down the road, they saw a nice looking restaurant that featured breakfast. On the window in prominent letters the sign read, "Ham and eggs our specialty."

"Let's go there," said the chicken. But the pig was hesitant. "That's easy for you to say," he said, "All they want from you is a donation, from me they expect total commitment."

Total commitment occurs when the self is removed from the center of one's life. In the case of the pig or Napoleon's "Old Guard" that can be dangerous. With the artists Renoir and Kreisler, it means pain and self-sacrifice.

The Bright Side

Grace moves self from the center as well. As we give GRATITUDE to God for everything and RELEASE to God all that we have, part of that "all" is the self—the very center of our existence. When we let go of everything—even our center, our core (the pit)—then self is replaced at the center!

Such maturity in grace is rare. More often, spiritual maturity is like the four-year old at the pediatrician's office for a check up. As the doctor looked in her ears with an otoscope, he asked, "Do you think I'll find Big Bird in here?" The little girl stayed silent. Next, the doctor took a tongue depressor and looked down her throat. He asked, "Do you think I'll find the Cookie Monster down there?" Again, the little girl was silent. Then the doctor put a stethoscope to her chest. As he listened to her heart beat, he asked, "Do you think I'll hear Barney in there?" "Oh, no!" the little girl replied. "Jesus is in my heart. Barney's on my underpants."

It's a lot easier having Barney on one's underpants than to have something other than self in one's heart—at the center.

Grace that is so strong and that has given up all with empty, praying hands, can receive everything with cross-embossed ACCEPTING hands. With grace at the center of one's life, then other people and God become more important. Receiving grace changes one's behavior because it changes one's center.

Giving up the center is the last thing most of us would want to do. We like being at the center and are extremely reluctant to give up the power that stems from the hub. We would like to reside at the nucleus of our lives instead of God's rule of grace. There is enormous risk in giving up and letting go.

But when a person is displaced by grace as the center of his or her universe, life changes. It is obvious in the kindly behavior and gracious, caring actions. If one has been flooded by grace, then one's words and actions engulf those around with graciousness. Sin is forgiven, kindness is practiced, love prevails. Grace has its effect. Even one's cat or dog should recognize the difference in the person genuinely seized by grace. A grace-filled person must be different in the same way the center of a peach is different from the center of an avocado. The center is revealed in the life that flows from that center.

The last holdout is usually one's purse. That is why the checkbook is a wonderful tool for checking one's center. It will reveal and measure priorities and values more than any other tool. Anybody can see your values by examining your checkbook! If a biographer really wanted to know you, he or she might check your birth record and talk to your friends and family members and seek to learn your history. But if the biographer really wanted to *know* YOU, he or she would need to read that book that best reveals your values. Your biographer would have to see your checkbook to know the real you. Jesus put it like this: "For where your treasure is, there will your heart be also."58

Commitment to grace shows itself in your actions, your thoughts, your attitudes and your checkbook. Everyone knows your values if they think about it or care to ask enough questions.

The prayerful life of grace maintains a posture of COMMITMENT represented by hands holding other hands. The self has moved off the center. It's time to reach out. Now grace sits where self once sat. Grace-filled commitment is where grace reigns and reaches out to God and others.

An ironic thing happens to those who give up their center: as they lose their lives they find them! Here is the way Jesus put it: "those who want to save their life will lose it, and those who lose their life for my sake will save it. What does it profit them if they gain the whole world, but lose or forfeit themselves?"[59]

Each of us should ask, "Who or what is at the center of my life?" More than likely the answer is not God's grace (the cross). It probably will be self. But self is a small package. Why not open up to the huge universe of God's grace? Listen to what Jesus said:

"No good tree bears bad fruit, nor again does a bad tree bear good fruit; for each tree is known by its own fruit. Figs are not gathered from thorns, nor are grapes picked from a bramble bush. The good person out of the good treasure of the heart produces good, and the evil person out of evil treasure produces evil; for it is out of the abundance of the heart that the mouth speaks."[60]

Whatever is at the center will show its self in how the rest acts. At the center of a peach is a peach pit. First came the pit—then came the peach. You won't find apple seeds in the center of a peach. You won't find a pine cone in the center of a peach. You will find, in the center of a good peach, a pit. Just like Jesus said.

Most people are committed to themselves or their families. Some are devoted to their jobs. Others are committed to their communities and some to their church. But as for you, dear child of the heavenly Father, let your center be the grace that brought you forth and that brought you to this time and this place for a special reason. And let your commitment be to the God of grace and to those who join you in mission to make this a grace-filled world.

Join with others and be the great and glorious being you were called by God to be.

I find it significant that Jesus, when he taught his disciples to pray, taught them to pray in community: *Our* Father, he said. "Give *us* this day our daily bread and forgive *us* our sins as we forgive those who sin against us. Lead *us* not into temptation but deliver *us* from evil..."

Most of us would never have thought to make such a prayer so community oriented so that even the necessary forgiveness of sins and reconciliation rests with our ability to do the same with one another. We are truly called to hold hands together and live together because in Christ we are all brother and sister—family.

Last summer I had an incredible two days. One day I went to the coastal area of northern California and witnessed the grandeur of the giant coastal redwoods. These soaring behemoths are the tallest living things that have ever existed. And my eyes saw those glorious plants! It is hard for me to imagine a tree that grows as tall as the United State's capitol building in Washington, D.C. But the coastal redwoods grow that tall!

The next day I went into the foothills of the Sierra and saw the giant Sequoias. Related to the coastal redwoods they are not as tall but they are more massive and hence more impressive! The giant Sequoias are the most massive living things ever created. And I saw these beauties with my own eyes! They exist here in my own lifetime!

Now what enables these wonders of nature to grow to such massive volume and such towering heights is that they have an interconnected, underground root system that gives each tree the freedom to soar.

The same is true for us. As we throw our lives into the hands of God in the prayerful life of grace, we grow to our highest and attain our greatness by the interconnections we have with others who support us and pray for us and listen to us and talk with us. These fellow redwoods give us all we need to soar. Commit and commune! Lose your life so that you might find it. Go in grace! Grow in grace! Give your life to something so much larger than itself. And may grace be your center, your guide, your all.

Go ahead, join hands with others in the prayerful life of grace. Join hands with God and commit all yourself and all your ways to the God who loves you so. Go ahead and join your hands with other grace-bearers in a cause the world desperately needs to learn about: GRACE!

CHAPTER SIX

▼

ENTHUSIASM & ENJOYMENT
(The Posture of Upraised Hands)

I know that there is nothing better for them than to be happy and enjoy them-selves as long as they live; moreover, it is God's gift that all should eat and drink and take pleasure in all their toil. I know that whatever God does endures for-ever; nothing can be added to it, nor anything taken from it; God has done this, so that all should stand in awe before him. (Ecclesiastes 3:12-14)

The *E* of GRAC*E* could easily stand for *Enthusiasm* which is a beautiful word meaning, "in God." *En-theos* is certainly something that grace brings about. Being *En-theos* reflects the center, the core of faith and *Commitment*. But there is something deeper. Being *in God* results in an inner joy. So the word I like is *Enjoy-ment!*

Enjoy like *enthusiasm* is the resultant gift of grac<u>E</u>. An enthusiastic person, whether at a ball game or lively praise service often raises his or her hands in a victorious gesture that also happens to be an ancient form of prayer—our fifth gesture of prayer.

Aunt Martha had both joy and enthusiasm:

LETTER FROM AUNT MARTHA

Got a letter from Aunt Martha the other day. She writes…

> The other day I went up to a local Christian bookstore and saw a "honk if you love Jesus" bumper sticker. I was feeling particularly sassy that day because I had just come from an uplifting Bible study preceded by a thrilling choir rehearsal the night before, so I bought the sticker and put it on my bumper. Boy, I'm glad I did! What an uplifting experience that followed!

> I was stopped at a red light at a busy intersection, just lost in thought about the Lord and how good God is …and I didn't notice that the light had changed. It is a good thing someone else loves Jesus because if he hadn't honked, I'd never have noticed! I found that LOTS of people love Jesus! Why, while I was sitting there, the guy behind started honking like crazy, and then he leaned out of his window and screamed, "For the love of GOD! GO! GO!" What an exuberant cheerleader he was for Jesus!

> Everyone started honking! I just leaned out of my window and started waving and smiling at all these loving people. I even honked my horn a few times to share in the love! There must have been a man from Florida back there because I heard him yelling something about a "sunny beach"…I saw another guy waving in a

funny way with only his middle finger stuck up in the air. Then I asked my teenage son in the back seat what that meant, he said that it was probably a Hawaiian good luck sign or something. Well, I've never met anyone from Hawaii, so I leaned out the window and gave him the good luck sign back.

My son burst out laughing...why, even he was enjoying this religious experience! A couple of the people were so caught up in the joy of the moment that they got out of their cars and started walking towards me. I bet they wanted to pray or ask what church I attended, but this is when I noticed the light had changed. So, I waved to all my sisters and brothers grinning, and drove on through the intersection. I noticed I was the only car that got through the intersection before the light changed again and I felt kind of sad that I had to leave them after all the love we had shared, so I slowed the car down, leaned out of the window and gave them all the Hawaiian good luck sign one last time as I drove away.

Praise the Lord for such wonderful folks![61]

Aunt Martha seems to be enjoying her faith. Joy is the result of the prayerful life of grace. St. Paul says it well: *Rejoice in the Lord always; again I will say, Rejoice.*[62] As we have noted earlier, the very word GRACE has its root in the Latin *gratia* which itself is a direct translation of the Greek *charis* which means, "I rejoice." (for our purposes: "enjoy!")

Joy is not a word in common usage in our modern English tongue perhaps because the concept of joy is so rarely enjoyed. Social scientists over the last three decades have written some 46,000 papers on depression but a scant 400 on joy.[63] Dr. Martin Seligman, University of Pennsylvania psychologist and past president of the American Psychological Association, in a 1998 speech said, "Social science now finds itself in almost total darkness about the qualities that make life most worth living."[64]

It is a sad commentary that the focus on the negatives of life reflected by secular social science is associated with modern religious life as well. Many people do not expect to find joy in anything religious. Religious people have often been guilty of showing anything but joy. Judgment? Yes. Condemnation? Of course. Seriousness? Expected. Most people have met religious folks who seem as far removed from joy as the sun from a star-lit sky.

Religious people lack joy because of the seriousness of their condition. Pious folks know that God is holy and pure and that human nature is sinfull. In the battle against sin, there is no room for joy. Try to keep the demands of the law. Try for one day to follow the stringent letter of the law laid down in the Sermon on the Mount.[65]

The righteousness of God's perfect law rules out all joy—except by grace. As G.K. Chesterton has put it somewhere, "No man can be joyful except the serious man. The thing called high spirits is only possible to the spiritual. Ultimately a man cannot rejoice in anything except the nature of things: a man can enjoy nothing except religion."[66]

It is humanly impossible to live a perfect life and yet most of us believe that if anyone could do it, we *could* if only we *would*. So some human beings (those generally branded as "religious") embark on a journey of perfection—holiness. But pursuit of a perfect life often has a serious side-effect: solemnity, gravity, sobriety—deadly seriousness and, quite often, the air of supremacy and, pride (which has been called one of the "deadly sins".

Many non-religious people would be surprised to hear how often words such as "joy" or "rejoice" or "blessed" are found in the pages of the Bible.

The word "joy" for example is found 172 times in some 162 verses of the Bible! "Rejoice" occurs 147 times in 141 verses! "Blessed" is even more prevalent: 259 times in 244 verses.

The biblical word for "exultant joy" was a new word writers of the Bible had to invent because the language of the day was not expressive enough to represent the joy that the Hebrew God of salvation could bring.[67]

Included in the word "joy" are English cognates such as optimism, gladness, pleasure, hilarity and happiness. The very word GRACE has its root in the original Greek which means, "I rejoice. I am glad." Furthermore, it is this very root word for joy that is most common in the New Testament! Grace and joy are intimately connected. William Morrice, who published an exhaustive word study of the word *joy* in the New Testament, says, "the whole message of the New Testament is good news of great joy for all people (cf. Luke 2:10). Christianity is a message of joy from beginning to end."[68]

The skeptic (or realist) might legitimately ask, how can a person rejoice and be glad with so much sin, death and darkness? How can there be rejoicing when there is so much pain and sickness? How can the poor in spirit be blessed? How can those who mourn find relief and even joy? How can those who are meek or seeking righteousness in a sin-filled world find blessing? Clearly joy comes by God's grace. Grace alone. Outward evidence for any genuine basis for joy is lacking. Inward, spiritual evidence for genuine joy is precluded—by grace.

THE DARK SIDE

Honestly, have you ever met a person who didn't want to be happy? Don't we all want happiness? Don't we all share that common thread? Every person wants what is best for him or herself. The only people I know who might not want the best are those beaten down people who deeply believe they don't deserve it. But even they came to this conclusion after having first believed they wanted happiness. At root don't we all want to be happy? I believe so.

If this is the case, why are so many people so miserable? Why so many unhappy people? Why does drug abuse abound? Why are our communities tethered by crime? Why so much fear? Why the worry? Why anger and resentment? Why is depression so rampant? Why the incredible misery? Somehow, some way, something has gone wrong!

The problem is two-fold: we seek happiness under the mistaken assumption that happiness, like most anything else, can be sought and found. Secondly, in our seeking, we look in all the wrong places.

All of us want happiness and many of us pursue it fervently. Some seek happiness in pleasure. It is easy to equate pleasure with happiness. Pleasure feels good. Happiness feels good. So we clamor for entertainment. "Entertain me," we say. "Give me my favorite music group. I want all their cd's...." "Entertain me. Give me a good, thrilling movie. Satisfy me with a good love story. Make me laugh with a good comedy."

Fatty, salty food tastes so good and therefore feels good. We look for pleasure in the food we eat and the result is that half of all Americans are overweight! We look for satisfaction of our sense of aesthetics and want the newest and best car money can buy. We want all the comforts a home can provide: cable television, a computer linked to the internet, and a perfectly manicured lawn. We look for a spacious kitchen and multiple bathrooms with luxurious baths. The average home size keeps growing. The accumulation of things that will pleasure us mushrooms.

The pleasure seeker always finds there is something about being a couch potato that is not ultimately satisfying. In fact there is an irony at work here: the more we seek pleasure and satisfaction, the more it eludes us! That doesn't make rational sense. But it is true.

The sex industry is thriving as pornography shoulders every legitimate form of internet, video and magazine enterprise. But when sex becomes the center of one's life, then boredom sets in. While sex is a powerful human urge, it is clear we are meant for higher purposes. The pleasure of illicit sex is quickly extinguished by guilt, disease, pregnancy and family breakup. Most people, allowing their sexual urges to dominate their lives, find regret—much of it with life-long consequences.

Lord Byron is perhaps a classic example of a life lived for pleasure. In his short life, he sought every form of pleasure and yet wrote: "The worm, the canker, and grief are mine alone." Most pleasure-seekers can relate to his voice of despair. The pursuit of pleasure results in misery.

How many of us dream of hitting it big in Vegas or winning the lottery? When we hear a news report about a common, ordinary person who wins big, we think, "What if that had been me?" It is an unspoken assumption that money equals happiness. Since the shortage of money causes so much misery, it only stands to reason that money will solve most, if not all, human problems. But the world is littered with lottery winners who would gladly go back to the days when they had more true friends and fewer things.

Throughout history money and the things money can buy have been God's major competitors. Jesus said a person cannot love money and God—"(Instead) store up for yourselves treasures in heaven, where neither moth nor rust consumes and where thieves do not break in and steal."[69] Paul writes, "the love of money is a root of all kinds of evil."[70]

Money and its accouterments bring on numerous worries and fears. I was talking to a man the other day who works for a large pharmaceutical company that has developed an anti-anxiety medication. "Business is great," he said. "The more the economy roars along, the more we sell. We love to see people get wealthy off the stock market." The wealthier people get, the more they need the anxiety remedy.

I can attest in my own life that money does not bring happiness. And neither does the lack of money bring joy. In fact the lack of money can bring great grief. When I was a young father, I was paid such a low salary that I could not provide properly for my family. For awhile, I had to use credit cards to make ends meet. Obviously that is a dead-end street and does not last long. As our family welfare spiraled down, my anxiety over not having money increased. I, too, fantasized that all I really needed was more money.

So I set out to do better and to get a little more money. My salary doubled. Then doubled yet again. But enough was never enough. I always seemed about ten percent short! "If I just made ten-percent more," I would say to myself, "*then* we could do really well."

The promise that money would solve all my problems has caused me more anxiety and grief than any other element of my life. I suspect the same is true for countless others.

As a product of our culture, I constantly must resist the lure of wanting more and thinking that more will satisfy. Money does not and cannot ultimately satisfy. Nearly all of us can affirm the truism that there are many wealthy people who are abjectly miserable. But somehow most of us think that we could handle wealth if just given the chance. "That wouldn't happen to me," we say.

Jay Gould, the American millionaire (in days when millionaire had today's equivalency of billionaire), had plenty of money in his life. When dying, he said: "I suppose I am the most miserable man on earth." Money and things do not guarantee happiness. In fact the pursuit of money and things will bring unhappiness. Materialism cannot satisfy what is, at root, a spiritual hunger and thirst.

Many turn to status and position—success—as their savior from misery. People will give their entire lives to their company because they need to prove that they are people of worth and that they are a success. They have no time for significant relationships. They have no time for God and the kingdom of grace. All they have is the job. And as the years go by and they climb upward and reach the top rung of a long ladder, they find the ladder is against the wrong building.

I have always been amazed at what we human beings will do to receive attention. A young child will deliberately knock over the lamp if she is ignored too long. A grown man will swallow swords. A fully adult woman will walk a tight-rope over Niagara Falls. Success and the attention it attracts says to the world and the self, "I am worthy! I am somebody!"

Lord Beaconsfield enjoyed more than his share of both success and position. He had proven himself. Yet he wrote: "Youth is a mistake; manhood a struggle; old age a regret." All the attention in the world cannot bring happiness and joy. Fleeting moments? Yes. Lasting significance? Never.

People love glory and see glory as the road to worthiness. In modern times the road to glory is often vicarious through sports. We are exhilarated (yes, even happy) when our team wins and devastated (or at least sad) when our team loses. Today's athlete lives a glorious life and we reward such lives with our rapt attention and our dollars. They win our happiness by their glory.

During war, military glory supplants sports. Alexander the Great conquered the known world in his day. Having done so, this young man allegedly wept in his tent, before he said, "There are no more worlds to conquer."

There is an illusion that celebrity brings memory as well as recognition. In fact, memory becomes far more important than recognition as celebrity often brings too much recognition. The following came to me as an apt illustration of the futility of trying to achieve recognition or immortality via memory:

> Now I see why powerful people often wear sunglasses-the spotlight blinds them to reality. They suffer from a delusion that power means something (it doesn't). They suffer from the misconception that titles make a difference (they don't). They are under the impression that earthly authority will make a heavenly difference (it won't).

> Can I prove my point? Take this quiz.
> Name the ten wealthiest people in the world.
> Name the last ten Heisman trophy winners.
> Name the last ten winners of the Miss America contest.
> Name eight people who have won the Nobel or Pulitzer prize.
> How about the last ten Academy Award winners for best picture or the last decade's worth of World Series winners?

> How did you do? I didn't do well either. With the exception of you trivia hounds, none of us remember the headliners of yesterday too well.

> Surprising how quickly we forget, isn't it? And what I've mentioned above are no second-rate achievements. These are the best in their

fields. But the applause dies. Awards tarnish. Achievements are forgotten. Accolades and certificates are buried with their owners.

Here's another quiz. See how you do on this one:
Think of three people you enjoy spending time with.
Name ten people who have taught you something worthwhile.
Name five friends who have helped you in a difficult time.
List a few teachers who have aided your journey through school.
Name half-a-dozen heroes whose stories have inspired you.

Easier? It was for me, too. The lesson? The people who make a difference are not the ones with the credentials, but the ones with the concern.

"People don't care how much you know. People just want to know how much you care."[71]

So we look for happiness and it cannot be purchased or achieved. The right to the pursuit of happiness always remains a right and not a reality. Happiness cannot be found in any lasting respect primarily because joy is the result of the prayerful, grace-filled life, not the pursuit. The Declaration of Independence may seek for each person the right to "the pursuit of happiness," but happiness and joy are results, not aims. Those things we mistakenly view as means to happiness: pleasure, money, fame, position and glory will possibly bring fleeting wisps of happiness, but they cannot bring the real thing. They do not bring joy. Joy comes. It happens!

THE BRIGHT SIDE

One of our neighbors saw a white turtle dove in her yard and she beckoned it to come to her. To her utter amazement, the dove flew to her and alit on her finger. Joy is a lot like that dove. It comes and it comes surprising.

A person would not expect a dove to land in her hand. Likewise the surprise of sudden joy is wonderful, usually unexpected and quite the opposite of finding joy. Who is most likely to receive such delightful joy? More often than not the person using his or her life in service to something larger than self is also the person most likely to experience the divine gift of joy. Pleasure, power, sex, glory, money—none of these bring ultimate happiness or joy. All are over-rated.

George Bernard Shaw said it so very well:

> "This is the true joy in life, the being used for a purpose recognized by yourself as a mighty one: the being thoroughly worn out before you are thrown on the scrap heap, and being a force of nature instead of a feverish selfish little clod of ailments and grievances, complaining that the world will not devote itself to making you happy."[72]

The joy of living comes when we find a noble purpose and live in the state of God's grace. The prayerful life of grace will point each person in the direction of JOY. The lost is found!

How to explain it? Impossible. Just imagine:

I once had a colleague who participated in a real life drama that resulted in pure joy. As a minister he was called to the home of an active family who were members of the church. They had just received devastating news. Indeed the news was shocking. The couples' beautiful, 22 year-old daughter, had died apparently at her own hands! "This just doesn't make sense," the mother said to her pastor between sobs of inconceivable grief. "She had everything to live for. She gave no signs what-so-ever that she was considering suicide."

After a period of frantic telephone calls to relatives and as arrangements were being made for the funeral, the family was invited to come to the county morgue to identify the body. The pastor went along for support. He saw the body rolled out and the sheet taken from the body. Against the best of hope, as the sheet was rolled back from the face of the body, all could see it was the beloved daughter. Her beautiful blond hair curled gently around the pearl-white chin. The daughter had died and it was apparently suicide. She had jumped from the eighth floor of an apartment building. She was dressed in her signature blue jeans. It was Holly all right. She was dead.

When the family returned home, the telephone began to ring as people learned of the family tragedy. Then after answering one phone call the mother shrieked, "Holly! That can't be you." It was. The daughter was fine. The body all had identified was not the beloved daughter they thought. It was a classic case of mis-identification on a scale beyond fiction. Imagine the joy! Imagine the happiness! Grief only came in the knowledge that someone, somewhere had lost a beautiful daughter.

We know something of that joy because a man came to live among us. He taught with great wisdom and dealt with all people as a deeply compassionate soul. He died a real death. But on the third day he rose again. "Why do you look for the living among the dead?" they asked. "He is not here, he is risen."

And we respond, HE IS RISEN INDEED!

Though death lap at our doorstep, we can have joy because we know the ending: CHRIST IS RISEN! ("He is risen indeed!")

Several years ago I was privileged to know and come to love and deeply respect a member of my parish who was a wizened-haired patriarch named Elmer Danielson. For forty years he and his wife Lillian had served as missionaries in Tanzania, Africa. This couple and their family had one stark, defining moment in their lives and that moment centered on the resurrection.

Elmer had gone to Africa in 1928. There he met his sweetheart, Lillian. Soon they married with a marriage based on a love for the Lord and for each other. They also soon had five children. In 1939 they traveled back to the United States for furlough. Their youngest and sixth child was born in the United States on May 1 of 1939. In early 1940, Elmer felt called to return to what was then known as Tanganyika (modern day Tanzania) alone—leaving his family behind in America because of the troubling clouds of war gathering on the horizon.

A lonely husband and father on the hot plains of Africa thrilled at the news that a whole boatload of missionaries—including his beloved Lillian and their six children—would be traveling to Africa that very spring via the Egyptian freighter Zamzam. Mom and kids left New York harbor in March and headed to South America before traversing the South Atlantic. After they left South American heading for Africa while in the middle of the ocean, a German war ship shelled the Zamzam. She sank in only a few minutes.

Elmer was troubled that some 53 days had passed since the boat left New York. On Sunday, May 19, he was on the Wembere Plains attending a dying man though the night. Early the next morning, fellow missionary Stan Anderson and his wife Ruth arrived. Ruth told Elmer that Stan wanted to speak to him outside. As Elmer reported,

> Stan's face was broken in lines and by tears, and his voice would hardly work. He hadn't slept all night. He took me by the arm, and while walking me around the courtyard, fitfully said: 'The

Zamzam was reported over last night's radio as long overdue at Capetown, and it is feared it has been sunk by enemy actions.' In fact, the news was that everybody was considered lost.

Elmer's response was immediate and filled with emotion:

> Who could grasp anything as terrible as that in a brief moment? But moment by moment the anguish grew until my world was inky black. My heart broke and cried out to God: 'No! No! No! It can't be so! It is too terrible! It is too much! That bravest mother and sweetheart and precious six little kiddies, innocent, hopeless, all gone!

The week passed with great anxiety. The man Elmer had been attending died. Even though he could not feel up to the task, Elmer's job was to conduct the funeral. "I didn't want to go," he said, "but a voice said: 'Go!' Can I bury Mac when my own heart is in anguish over my loved ones? What peculiar circumstances under which to hear such tragic family news!"

As Elmer prepared his message based on Jesus and widow of Nain's son showing Jesus' compassion for the sorrowing, and His power over death. He asked, "Was that His (God's) message to me, too, that day? I wanted these mine workers to get a clear message from Jesus, as they seldom had a chance to hear." But Elmer's sermon preparation was interrupted: "The door opened and Ruth entered, joyfully exclaiming: 'They're saved. They've been landed on French soil. Mr. Haman will tell you more. He heard it last night over the 10 o'clock broadcast from Germany.'"

As you can imagine Elmer was filled with emotion. "And could I dance there for joy—at a funeral?" he asked.

Elmer's tragic loss turned to triumphant joy. Not only did his family survive, but the entire crew and passengers of the Zamzam survived. There was not one fatality despite constant shelling and the sinking of the ship. Lillian and her young crew of six children were in the waters of the South Atlantic because their lifeboat, hit with shrapnel from the shelling, sank beneath them.

Elmer wrote in his diary concerning May 19-26, Monday to Monday— "What a week—brought to the depths of agony and raised to the plane of hope. The hand of the Father shows through it—and much remains to be revealed. Precious, dearest, bravest sweetheart and mother—I love you. Precious, God-given, bravest little kiddies—I love you! Father, I cry, unite us to serve Thee together. Thy will be done!"[73]

Can or should a person dance at a funeral? The answer seems to hinge upon the very power of grace. Is the resurrection real? Is hope genuine? If it is then dancing and joy are most appropriate—at a funeral, at work, at home—everywhere! ENJOY!

Astonishingly, no one perished on the Zamzam and the family survived. It was a case of despair, hope and resurrection triumph. But while I was Elmer and Lillian's pastor, I conducted both their funerals. They had long, productive, joy-bent lives, but death still came and their earthly life ended. The Psalmist says, "Weeping may linger for the night, but joy comes with the morning."[74]

The simple affirmation of Easter makes all the difference in the world because if we can know that life triumphs over death, then we can most certainly have joy and even the ravages of death cannot take that away. If grace is real and God accepts us as we are and loves us and cares about us, then that makes a great difference.

I like the way the Psalmist put it:

> O LORD, you have searched me and known me. You know when I sit down and when I rise up; you discern my thoughts from far away. You search out my path and my lying down, and are acquainted with all my ways. Even before a word is on my tongue, O LORD, you know it completely. You hem me in, behind and before, and lay your hand upon me. Such knowledge is too wonderful for me; it is so high that I cannot attain it. Where can I go from your spirit? Or where can I flee from your presence? If I ascend to heaven, you are there; if I make my bed in Sheol, you are there. If I take the wings of the morning and settle at the farthest limits of the sea, even there your hand shall lead me, and your right hand shall hold me fast. If I say, "Surely the darkness shall cover me, and the light around me become night," even the darkness is not dark to you; the night is as bright as the day, for darkness is as light to you. For it was you who formed my inward parts; you knit me together in my mother's womb. I praise you, for I am fearfully and wonderfully made. Wonderful are your works; that I know very well. My frame was not hidden from you, when I was being made in secret, intricately woven in the depths of the earth. Your eyes beheld my unformed substance. In your book were written all the days that were formed for me, when none of them as yet existed. How weighty to me are your thoughts, O God! How vast is the sum of them! I try to count them—they are more than the sand; I come to the end—I am still with you.[75]

God knows us before we could ever know ourselves. God knew about you when the words of this Psalm were penned to parchment some 2900 years ago! God will know about you 2900 or 2.9 million years hence. How can we understand the depth of God's knowledge of us? We might as well count the grains of sand on all the shores of all the seas and all the lakes and rivers of the world. But when all the grains are counted, we will have only started to understand the mind of God and God's amazing grace.

Why human and animal suffering? Why misery? Why such seemingly pointless pain? All are questions raised by finite minds probing the infinite mind of God. So many of our prayers are answered with, "Not yet." We do not yet know the answer to our most disturbing questions. But we can hold on to that one sure thing that the prayerful life of grace offers us: GRACE. And that is enough for us until the answers are fully known. It is, as Paul explained, as if we peer into a mirror (which, in ancient times consisted of polished metal) that may be badly tarnished. The day is coming when we shall see "face to face."[76]

What happens to people when they experience great joy? The fifth posture of prayer is the posture of hands raised high overhead in the triumphant sign of joy and victory. The great game of life has been won! It is truly the "World Series" to beat all World Series. It is the triumph of the ages. Death has been defeated and the victory is God's. The grave has lost its power. Doubt has vanished. Love has conquered. It is the posture of the great "YES!" (in the language of the Bible that great YES! is "AMEN!").

CHAPTER SEVEN

▼

PRACTICAL APPLICATION OF THE PRAYERFUL POS- TURES OF GRACE

But the seventh day is a sabbath to the LORD your God; you shall not do any work—you, your son or your daughter, your male or female slave, your livestock, or the alien resident in your towns. For in six days the LORD made heaven and earth, the sea, and all that is in them, but rested the seventh day; therefore the LORD blessed the sabbath day and consecrated it. (Exodus 20:10-11)

How can the prayerful life of grace and the postures of grace help me in my daily life? Daily prayer is a start. Prayer is central to the life and practice of any person seeking deeper spiritual realities regardless of his or her faith. Most people reach a certain spiritual milestone, aware that the world is larger than what meets the senses. Most people have spiritual occasions when they almost cannot help but pray. Profound gratitude, for example, erupts into prayer. When joy bursts upon a person, the natural response is reverential or exuberant prayer. In times of desperation, "there are no atheists in foxholes," as frightened human beings plead their desolate cases to their definition and perception of God. In times of intense loneliness, the deepest part of human nature speaks of spiritual companionship. Prayer emanates at some time or another in most people's lives.

When the habit of prayer becomes conscious and deliberate (instead of reaction to momentary circumstances), then the practice of prayer leads the individual to paths of deeper spirituality. The various postures of the prayerful life of grace is a discipline of deliberate, conscious, willful prayer that has structure built around the Christian concept of grace.

In no way does the practice of the prayerful life of grace indicate superior faith or favor with God (otherwise it would not be grace). The prayerful life of grace, utilizing the postures of prayer as an aid, serves only to enhance the spiritual practices of the participant. It reminds the practitioner of the various aspects of grace and that grace begins with the individual but continually expands to include the community, the world and the universe.

St. Paul tells the Thessalonians, "pray without ceasing."[77] And, indeed, spiritually oriented people do find themselves praying day and night; at home and away; lying down and standing up; before and after meals; before and after work. There is no place where prayer is not entirely appropriate. For most people, place and posture tend to be spontaneous and not disciplined and deliberate. To attempt a prayerful life of grace, there are several obvious aids: posture, a quiet space (although certainly prayer can be used in any and all circumstances.) A regular time is usually beneficial and many find closed eyes and a comfortable position advantageous.

The prevailing mythology says that these busy, noisy times, make the quiet more difficult to find. One of the outcomes of a prayerful life of grace is the discovery that our worth does not depend upon our busy lives or our achievements. Grace is gift—free and undeserved. Worth is not based on "net worth" and value is not something achieved, earned or proven—but given.

Earlier times paid more attention to the human need for a seventh day of rest and being (versus doing). We are, after all, human *beings*, NOT human *doings*. Today we are so concerned about activity and achievement (thereby proving our worth) that we imagine and convince ourselves that we don't have time to take a day of rest and re-creation (in the truest sense of re-creating our inner selves). The simple observance of the commandment to "Remember the sabbath day, and keep it holy"[78] may be exactly what we need to live in grace. The word "sabbath" is the Hebrew word for "seventh." The ancient wisdom proves true even today—every seventh day we need to rest and live in grace alone. On the seventh day we don't have to prove ourselves. On the day of rest we can "keep it holy" (and the word "holy" means "set aside," "special").

Holy days, holy moments within each day, bring us back to our spiritual center. I find it fascinating that one of the Ten Commandments is a command to rest but there no commandment to work! It is all too easy to work. It takes no convincing that work is necessary if we are to survive. But one imagines that life can continue without consequence by neglecting the rest, peace and quiet of grace.

GRATITUDE: FOLDED HANDS; THANKFUL HEART

So, take your hands and fold them. Take time right now for thanksgiving. Human life is shaped by thought and those who think thankful thoughts tend to find increasingly more for which to be thankful. Gratitude, as someone has written, is not only the greatest of virtues but the parent of all others. It is the first posture of grace.

If, in the busy-ness of daily living you get no further than the folded hands of gratitude, you will have attained more lasting value, more quality, than most people get working twelve-hour days and seven day weeks. How blessed is the person who begins and ends each day with gratitude. How fortunate the one cultivating an attitude of prayer throughout the day. How rich the life suffused with gratitude even for the little things that come in the moments that make for daily life.

When thinking thankful thoughts, the natural tendency is to be thankful for life's various gains. However, life consists of both gains and losses. It is easy and natural to celebrate the gains, but the losses are often more difficult. It is important to be thankful for all we have and all our gains and victories, but it is also important not to denigrate the need to grieve life's on-going losses.

Loss happens at every age. For the child the grieving is for childhood innocence. For the adult, grief comes from passing days and lost opportunities. As we age, we grieve loved ones who die and ultimately come to that point where we grieve our own deaths as we are forced to let go of all the people and things we have known and loved and must say "good bye" because our time also has run its course.

What if we could begin each day imagining that we had already lost all and died? Imagine entering each day's opening scenes, and finding those things we thought we had lost. With thankfulness we realize that our hearts are still beating and we have a body. We begin to understand that we have time and moments in which to live, move, love and fulfill purposeful lives. We comprehend that the loved ones we so easily take for granted are still with us and still give us opportunity to love them.

Joy cannot help but come to us when we begin to see not our troubles and pain but our opportunities and stewardship of what is ours right now: our bodies, our time, our loved ones, the various things we "own".

Take about three weeks of beginning and ending each day with the folded hands of gratitude. As time permits, begin imagining that what you have is new and found—as if for the first time. Your appreciation will grow as your thankfulness flourishes. Take about three weeks to think of the many things each day that come your way for which you are thankful. Intimately integrate your new-found attitude of gratitude into your life. Let your attitude of gratitude find its way into the center of your life.

If it is helpful, keep a diary or record of the times you began each day with the gesture of gratitude—folded hands. Do this for three weeks so that gratitude becomes a habit for you. Do take time at least once a week to imagine that everything begins lost and in a prayerful posture of folded hands, see those things come to you one at a time.

RELEASE: OPEN HANDS; EXPOSED LIFE

Oh how we want to cling. Babies cling to their mothers and are afraid to let go and face the cold and often cruel world. Mothers and fathers cling to their infants—afraid for them. But as time passes and the child matures, he or she establishes a unique personality and life. What is true in physical maturity is also true in spiritual growth. The prayerful life of grace embodies release because growth can continue only by release.

Sometimes just the posture of opening one's hands can help the process. With open hands, ask yourself, "What am I hanging on to which I needs release?" Ask the question with the full knowledge that you must let go of *everything*.

Here we are almost asking for something super-human. Why let go of *everything?* The great human tendency is to cling, "own", conserve and control. The last thing we want to do is let go of things, people, attitudes, feelings—life itself. But by letting go, and only by letting go, can we be positioned to receive life's greatest gift: grace.

Like the monkeys with clinched fists around a delicious treat inside a coconut shell, we cling to that which ultimately enslaves. True freedom comes from letting go. Let go and be free. All I can say is TRY IT.

Take a deep breath, close your eyes, release your hands as they lie on your lap and let go. Go through every area of your life: your past, present and future; your gilt, shame, and fears; your parents, children, and self; your possessions, money, things. Let go of all of it. RELEASE.

Letting go is surely one of life's toughest challenges. That is why it is so very hard to die. Have no illusions that letting go is easy—it is not. But with practice, it can be done. With practice you *can* let go of *everything*.

Try it—preferably after you have spent at least three weeks in GRATITUDE. Take your time learning to let go. I would suggest at least another three weeks of daily letting go. Dying takes time. Practice the difficult art of dying.

There is a wonderful consequence of prayerfully letting go. Doing so puts a person in deep contact with their spiritual and emotional selves. A person becomes aware of feelings—hurts, anger, fears, and so forth. This is particularly beneficial for men who often are incredibly out of touch with their emotional and spiritual natures.

Let go of all physical tension manifested in the body: tightness anywhere. Do a body scan starting at your feet and imagine going through your whole body scanning for stress and tension, particularly in muscles. Think of a machine or circle of light or whatever imagery is helpful starting at your feet and working all the way through your body to your head. It is scanning—sometimes slowly but always deliberately—looking for that tell tale tightness that says we don't want to let go. As your imaginary scan moves over your body, let go of any tension and let the muscles go flaccid. Think of your body as a dead weight as you let go and die. Don't let the heaviness surprise you. Dying is heavy business.

The hourglass is a helpful image and mechanism you can use to let go—with totally different results. Imagine the grains of an hourglass passing through from the upper chamber to the lower. The upper represents life yet to be lived. The lower stands for time past.

Now, with open hands, imagine those grains of sand passing through your hands. Feel them, let them flow between the fingers of each hand until you can feel no more grains. When you have reached the last grain and have given it all up, you have truly RELEASED everything to God.

Don't be surprised at the lightness you feel—almost a sensation of floating. It is only when we are able to release everything that we begin to understand how so many things we become attached to have been and are a burden—a weight—that drags our soul and keeps our spirit from soaring.

The moments, the minutes of letting go and the hours of disciplined release may be the most awesome spiritual awakening you will ever experience. Feel the grains flow like sand in an hourglass. Feel it—deeply—as you slowly die.

In the quietude of silence one can hear the "sound of sheer silence"[79] and the voice of God.

FURTHER RELEASE:

Now with your arms still at your side and palms up, name your shoulds and wishes. What *should* your life look like? How *should* people act? What *should* be the condition of the world? How *should* God operate? Begin with whatever is on your mind, "Dear, God, I wish life didn't pass so swiftly. I wish life did not have pain. I wish there were no illness or death. I wish people loved one another unconditionally. I wish I would love as I should. I wish…"

Allow yourself plenty of time to think of all the ways you wish things were different—in your opinion—better. Think of your life; the lives of those around you; the lives of people who suffer; the world. Much of our anger stems from the fact that things are not as we perceive they *should* be. Let your anger be a guide in what you wish were different.

Getting in deep touch with anger, frustration and life's greatest disappointments and illusions can be a lengthy process. For some of us these emotions have been simmering for many years and daily we add our most recent resentments to the brew.

Some people find it helpful to write down the *shoulds* of reality. "If I were God, these are the things I would do and this is how I would run the universe…"

With arms still at one's side, naming life's *shoulds* and *woulds* and every wish is the final stage of that difficult second posture of GRACE: *RELEASE.*

ACCEPTANCE: CROSSED ARMS; RECEIVING SPIRIT

Once you put your wishes on the table of the Lord, then you are in a position to more freely *ACCEPT* life as it is—on its own terms. When you have identified as many of the things you wish were so, then you are free to move your arms across your chest in a cruciform posture. Then you are in a position to *ACCEPT* life on its own terms.

Here is where the posture of the cross is helpful. The cross was a brutal instrument of death. Jesus chose the cross not because he wanted to suffer, but because it was God's inscrutable will. *WHY* God would demand a cross seemed strange and foreign even to Jesus. His desire was not the cross. "Let this cup pass from me," he fervently prayed in the Garden of Gethsemane.

Arms crossed over the chest helps us accept life as it is. There is much over which we have no control or understanding. This posture is for those things we must accept.

Accepting life as it is can be a most difficult task, but acceptance measures the maturity of a person as surely as a yardstick measures a person's height. And acceptance leads to something even better: God's love as it really is. With arms over the chest, allow those very arms to hug you. Imagine God's Spirit enfolding you into his will. Think of yourself as a precious, priceless, child of God. Allow yourself to be loved. Hear God say to you, "You are my own precious daughter," "You are my own beloved son."

How long one maintains this posture is up to the pray-er. You can maintain this posture for minutes and even hours, or but for a moment. Length of time is not important—attitude is supremely important. Allow yourself acceptance of life and acceptance of love.

The posture of acceptance of God's love is a great way to begin and end each day. Try it today. Begin this way; end the day this way. See if grace becomes more pervasive in your life by this simple act of allowing yourself to be loved.

Funny thing—when you allow God to love you, it spills over and you allow other people to love you as well. Perhaps most importantly, you allow yourself to love yourself! Imagine that!

COMMITMENT: LINKED ARMS; DEDICATED WILL

With prayerful hands joining other hands, link with others in the larger spiritual entity—the very body of Christ.

Throughout the New Testament, we are reminded that we are in community with others. There are no lone eagles out there worshipping in the solitude of nature. Despite our American penchant for rugged individualism, there is no room for it in the church. Solitary Christianity is an oxymoron. Christians *always* exist as part of a larger body, the body of Christ himself.

Jesus certainly patterned solitary prayer and lone times with God. How often he withdrew from the crowds to be alone with God. But Jesus also modeled the disciples' prayer: *"Our* Father…." The pray-er is part of a whole and yet still fully an individual—unique and precious to God.

Even in the solitude of prayer, Christians can link arms and join others. How? Prayer itself. Take time to pray for others. Praying for others might be the best thing you can do for yourself and others today.

Develop a prayer diary or prayer list that includes the names of all those you know and love as well as those you don't know and perhaps have trouble loving. What are the major concerns of the people you know? What health issues are they facing? What emotional burdens are they bearing? What psychological stress do they daily encounter? What family concerns are they dealing with? What are their fears? Worries? Dreams? Desires? What do you perceive might be God's will for them?

Love is as much a by-product of grace as gratitude. How can one so loved by God not love others? One can express love for others by practicing love in prayer. Ask yourself: What are the health concerns of others? What financial needs do they have? Who may be facing grave danger? Who is hurting because of a pending divorce? Who is feeling the pain of abject loneliness because of isolation in a nursing home? The needs of those around us are always there. As part of the very body of Christ, they become our needs as well.

Join hands in prayer. Yes, even in the privacy of your devotional life, join spiritual hands and commit yourself to the larger body of Christ. Link hand to hand in prayer. Let the visible posture of commitment to others link you around a dinner table, one on one in a nursing home, hand holding hand in worship.

I find it helpful to picture real people holding my hand when I am not with real people. If you are practicing the COMMITMENT posture of prayer in the solitude of your personal, devotional life, then picture and let your imagine feel the hands of people from your church or group who are united in the body of Christ, seeking his mission; his word of healing, love, and grace. Picture in your prayers the needs of others. This can be as involved as you want it to be.

You may picture someone with whom you have conflict. You may envision someone in great need of healing. You may see someone who is of the same mind as you and who seeks a world with more of God's grace.

The posture of grace can take moments or hours. It can be experienced in public (preferably) or in private. Experience the COMMITMENT of COMMUNITY.

ENJOYMENT: UPRAISED ARMS; EXUBERANT SOUL

The joy of grace moves hands in the victory position over the head! It seems to be a natural expression replicated at victorious athletic events, political rallies, and all public expressions of triumph. And what greater victory than grace? God's love freely given! Unconditional, unearned, and free—it can't get any better than that! So the hands linked in community and commitment freely move up in triumph and joy.

The forces of evil and death still operate. Pain, despair, loneliness, and human sin are as real as ever. The difference is grace. For the forces that would destroy our joy have already been annihilated even while they still operate.

The beauty of grace is its effectiveness as paradox. We may not be happy, but we can have joy. We may suffer the consequences of egregious human sin, yet forgiveness prevails. Our bodies are constantly dying, yet our souls are being refreshed daily with eternal life. While feeling most alone, one can sense great community. The less worthy we feel, the more grace operates.

Oh, there is reason for triumph and victory. The victory is ours. Raise your hands and shout for joy because grace triumphs!

Don't worry about how long to hold a posture—especially this one. Just as one would not normally end a great athletic contest with arms upraised for more than moments, so time is of little concern in this posture. The victorious hands of grace can be but a momentary gesture or they may be extended moments or minutes in praise to the God who graces us with love—free and undeserved.

There is great joy in praising our God of grace. Especially when you are with others, let this time come and go naturally. It would normally not be comfortable to have one's hands raised overhead for a prolonged time. Just ENJOY! Experience the ENTHUSIASM of God's dwelling among us and within us.

Prayers in the Judeo-Christian tradition end with the word, AMEN. While many may think it means, "the end," it really means something far more profound. Amen is a Greek word meaning simply *YES!* How very appropriate to end the prayerful postures of grace with the triumphant, certain, positive, simple word *YES!*

And sometimes that great affirmation is nothing more than a quiet smile upon the face. Let the great *YES!* have victory on your face right now.

The LORD bless you and keep you;
the LORD make his face to shine upon you *(smile)*, and be gracious to you; the LORD lift up his countenance upon you *(smile again)*, and give you peace.[80]

A PRAYER

Dear God, with hands folded in GRATITUDE, I lift my prayer of thanks to You. You have given me life and breath and the joy of living. You have given me this day—a day You have made. You have given me possessions for a time. You have given me people: family and friends. You have given me all good things. As I stop to think about it, thanks builds into thanksgiving and gratitude as my mind begins to comprehend all the good gifts from your gracious hand.

I open my hands to RELEASE all that I would possess. I tend to think all are mine, but they are not. All belongs to You, including myself, and I have a moment in time to use what is Yours.

I open my heart to the people You have used for blessing in my life. They too are not mine, they are Yours. I cannot control them. I can only love them. I RELEASE them now. I open my heart to the people who are different from me. To those whose ways and customs and beliefs are not mine.

I open my mind to ways of learning and perceiving that have never occurred to me before. I open my mind to your Spirit's movement in my world. I open my mind knowing that I cannot possibly comprehend the universe in all its magnitude. I cannot understand all Your ways, O Lord.

I open my soul to let go of all the anger that would consume me as well as the resentment that smolders like an ember. I open my soul to let go of the fear that sees the worst in things. How can I possibly know that what worries me now will come to pass? How can I possibly know that what seems serious now will not end in blessings yet unseen? I let go of my need to control outcomes.

My open hands fold to my shoulders as my arms cross my heart to ACCEPT. The crossed arms remind me of life's crosses all must bear. Life has its hurts and pain and we human beings are all on common ground. You have used the brutality of the cross as a sign that in the midst of all suffering, grace and Your eternal love triumph. I receive it in all humility.

May my self-hug remind me of Your love for me. You have taken me as I am, with all my shortcomings and sins and You have loved me with an eternal love. I receive what I can perceive and know that I can only begin to comprehend the depth of Your love for me.

My hands join other hands in community as my will COMMITS to larger purposes and greater life through community. I throw myself into that which I cannot alone accomplish but which, through the actions of others working in concert can, with me, accomplish. The greater WE *is* better than the solitary ME.

We join hands and become Your body, Your presence on this planet. We join hands and link arms in solidarity for the kingdom of grace You have given us to pursue.

Finally, with arms exuberantly raised, we ENJOY the grace we know defines our reality. With arms reaching to all the universe, we celebrate life! With joy we enter and close the day. With joy we shout the great "AMEN!" With joy we affirm "it shall be so!" YES!

Now—go with God in grace.

ENDNOTES

1 Paul Tillich, THE SHAKING OF THE FOUNDATIONS

2 Henri J. M. Nouwen, REACHING OUT.

3 From *Context,* (Vol. 27, Number 22, December 15, 1995) Martin E. Marty, Editor who quotes from *Review,* Summer, 1995, and the *Other Side*, September-October, 1995.

CHAPTER ONE

4 John 10:10. All biblical references from the New Revised Standard Version Bible, copyright © 1989, Division of Christian Education of the National Council of the Churches of Christ in the United States of America.

5 From HeroicStories, 5/18/1999, published by Freelance Communications, PO Box 17326, Boulder CO 80308, Randy Cassingham, Editor. Copyright 1999 HeroicStories.com, reprinted with permission. For free subscription information, see www.HeroicStories.com or e-mail Info@HeroicStories.com. Wayne (Tony) Mabes, author.

6 July 17, 2000, "Taking the mistakes out of medicine"

7 pg. 58

8 pg. 57

9 May, Gerald G. ADDICTION AND GRACE, Harper & Row, 1988, p. 17

10 Attributed to W.H. Murry of the Scottish Himalayan Expedition. I have not been able to verify the source of this quote. The couplet is that of Johann Wolfgang von Goethe (1749–1832), German poet, dramatist, novelist and scientist.

CHAPTER TWO

11 Frederick Langbridge, "A Cluster of Quiet Thoughts"

12 Philippians 4:11-13

13 THE COLLECTED WORKS OF ABRAHAM LINCOLN, Roy P. Basler, ed. Rutgers University Press: New Brunswick, New Jersey, 1953. According to Basler, the original draft of this proclamation has not been located. The version quoted is the most widely accepted, though there are versions of the proclamation which contain even more overt Christian references. One such version ends, "Intoxicated with unbroken success, we have become too self-sufficient to feel the necessity of redeeming and preserving grace, too proud to pray to the God that made us!" (William J. Wolf, THE ALMOST CHOSEN PEOPLE, Doubleday.)

14 Martin Rinkhart, 1586–1649; translated by Catherine Winkworth, 1829–1878.

15 Philippians 4:5

16 Romans 8:35-39

CHAPTHER THREE

17 Augustus M. Toplady

18 George MacDonald in Goerge MacDonald, AN ANTHOLOGY, edited by C.S. Lewis.

19 Genesis 1:28

20 Prayer by Reinhold Niebuhr and popularized by recovery groups—especially Alcoholics Anonymous.

21 Matthew 22:37-41 "He (Jesus) said to him (his questioner), 'You shall love the Lord your God with all your heart, and with all your soul, and with all your mind.' This is the greatest and first commandment. And a second is like it: 'You shall love your neighbor as yourself.' On these two commandments hang all the law and the prophets." It is clear from what Jesus said that sin stems not from prohibitions, inhibitions, good order or anything but love—of God, neighbor, self. At root sin is a violation against grace.

22 Attributed to Chad Walsh in a work entitled BEHOLD THE GLORY. I have not been successful in tracking down the author or the work.

23 Ephesians 4:31-32

24 Rev. Ted Peters cited by Willmar Thorkelson in "The Genes Made Me do It: Sin and Responsibility," *San Jose Mercury News,* Aug. 6, 1994, p. 10C.

25 *"Dynamic Preaching"* July, August, September. 1999, Vol. XIV, No. 3, p. 54

26 Ibid.

27 Johann Christoph Arnold, (Plough Publishing House, 1997), p. 51

28 *"Dynamic Preaching,"* Op. Cit.

29 William Hazlitt (1778–1830), english essayist, *Characteristics: In the Manner of Rochefoucault's Maxims,* no. 66 (1823; repr. In *The Complete Works of William Hazlitt,* vol. 9, ed. By P.P. Howe, 1932).

30 Matthew 5:30 "And if your right hand causes you to sin, cut it off and throw it away; it is better for you to lose one of your members than for your whole body to go into hell."

31 Donovan, Richard Niell. SermonWriter, March 18, 2001.

32 Adapted from a message by an unknown author sent by a friend.

33 Lewis, C. S., THE PROBLEM OF PAIN, Macmillan: NY, p. 93.

34 I have tried tracing the source of this quote and have not been successful. It is purportedly written by Ralph Beebe.

35 Ecclesiastes 3:6

36 Meister Eckhart, quoted in *Heirlooms*

37 Gibran, Kahlil, THE PROPHET, (NY: Alfred A. Knopf, 1934) p. 21

38 C. S. Lewis, THE FOUR LOVES, (NY: Harcourt Brace Jovanovich, 1960)

39 Yancey, Philip, WHAT'S SO AMAZING ABOUT GRACE? (Grand Rapids, MI: Zondervan Publishing House, 1997), p. 71

40 2 Corinthians 12:9

41 Adapted. Author unknown, sent via internet

CHAPTER FOUR

42 Matthew 5:3

43 An intimate address much like the childish "Daddy"

44 Mark 14:36

45 Literally, "scandal." Paul talks about the cross as the stumbling stone that repels so many people. It is the scandal that doesn't make sense. It is life on its own terms instead of ours.

46 1 Corinthians 1:22-23

47 John-Roger & Peter McWilliam, WEALTH 101, (Los Angeles, Prelude Press) pp. 149-155. Used with permission of the author.

48 Panati, Charles, EXTRAORDINARY ORIGINS OF EVERYDAY THINGS, (NY: Harper & Row), p. 38

49 From an e-mail sent by a friend. Attempts to find the ultimate source have not been successful. Attached comments by my friend.

50 Sounce unknown. Dr. Joshua Loth Liebman was rabbi of Temple Israel, Boston and one of the leading radio preachers in America before his untimely death in 1948 at the age of 41.

51 Book currently out of print

52 Source unknown

53 Hall, Thelma, TOO DEEP FOR WORDS, as quoted in *Christianity Today*, (July 10, 2000; Volume 44, No. 8), p. 45.

54 Augustine, SERMONS, as quoted in *Christianity Today*, (July 10, 2000; Volume 44, No. 8), p. 45.

55 Source unknown.

56 Deuteronomy 21:23

57 Philippians 4:7

CHAPTER FIVE

58 Matthew 6:21; Luke 12:34

59 For the text in its context: Luke 9:23-25

60 Luke 6:43-45

CHAPTER SIX

61 Anonymous. This quote came to me from friends via e-mail. I have seen several mutations of the same quote and cannot track down the original author.

62 Philippians 4:4

63 Terence Monmaney, *Los Angeles Times,* printed in *The Record (1/8/2000).*

64 Ibid.

65 Matthew 5-7

66 As quoted by William Morrice, JOY IN THE NEW TESTAMENT (Wm. B. Eerdmans Publishing Co.: Grand Rapids, MI, 1984), p. 48

67 E. Bevan, HELLENISM AND CHRISTIANITY (George Allen and Unwin, 1921), p. 72

68 William Morrice, JOY IN THE NEW TESTAMENT (Wm. B. Eerdmans Publishing Co.: Grand Rapids, MI, 1984), p. 75

69 Matthew 6:20

70 1 Timothy 6:10

71 Source unknown

72 George Bernard Shaw, quoted in COURAGE—YOU CAN STAND STRONG IN THE FACE OF FEAR, Jon Johnston, 1990, SP Publications, p. 171.

73 Danielson, Elmer R., FORTY YEARS WITH CHRIST IN TANZA-NIA: 1928–1968, Edited and Publshed by Eleanor (Danielson) Anderson, Rock Island, IL, 1996), pp. 58-59.

74 Psalm 30:5b

75 Psalm 139:1-18

76 1 Corinthians 13:12

CHAPTER SEVEN

77 1 Thessalonians 5:17

78 Exodus 20:8

79 1 Kings 19:12. The prophet Elijah stood before the mountain for a revelation from the Lord but God was not in the dramatic wind. Neither was the voice of God in the earthquake. Likewise God was not heard in the fire. But the voice of God came in what some translations say, "the still small voice" of God. (I Kings 19:11-12)

80 Numbers 6:24-26. This is the so-called Aaronic benediction used to close many Christian worship services.

0-595-22724-4

Made in the USA
Middletown, DE
25 October 2022

13478233R00083